T0119844

Lost and Found

COWLEY PUBLICATIONS is a ministry of the Society of Saint John the Evangelist, a religious community of men in the Episcopal Church. Emerging from the Society's tradition of prayer, theological reflection, and diversity of mission, the press is centered in the rich heritage of the Anglican Communion.

Cowley Publications seeks to provide books, audio cassettes, CDs, and other resources for the ongoing theological exploration and spiritual development of the Episcopal Church and others in the body of Christ. To this end, it is dedicated to developing a new generation of theological writers, encouraging them to produce timely, creative, and stimulating publications of excellence, and making these publications available widely, reaching both clergy and lay persons.

Lost and Found

adolescence, parenting,
and the formation of faith

Amanda Millay Hughes

Library of Congress Cataloging-in-Publication Data:
Hughes, Amanda Millay.
    Lost and found: adolescence, parenting, and the formation of
    faith / Amanda Millay Hughes.
        p. cm.
    ISBN 1-56101-207-6
    1. Christian education of teenagers. 2. Adolescence—Religious
    aspects——Christianity. I. Title.
    BV1475.9 .H84 2002
    268'.433—dc21

                                      2002013382

All scripture quotations, unless otherwise indicated, are taken from
the HOLY BIBLE, NEW INTERNATIONAL VERSION®.
NIV®. Copyright ©1973, 1978, 1984 by International Bible Society.
Used by permission of Zondervan. All rights reserved.

Four lines of "My House" by Nikki Giovanni reprinted by
permission of HarperCollins, Inc.

Cover design: Gary Ragaglia

This book is printed in the United States of America on acid-free
paper.

Cowley Publications
907 Massachusetts Ave.
Cambridge, Massachusetts 02139
800-225-1534 • www.cowley.org

Contents

Preface   vii

Introduction   1

chapter one
The Challenging Child   9

chapter two
The Problem with Identity   25

chapter three
The Community and the Culture   39

chapter four
The Time it Takes to Find   59

chapter five
The Search for Intimacy   79

chapter six
The Role of Elders   93

chapter seven
The Possibility of an Early Death   107

chapter eight
The Birth of Wisdom   131

chapter nine
Finding the Lost and Found   147

chapter ten
Toward a Theology of Parenting
and Adolescence   155

WHILE MAKING EVERY ATTEMPT to respect my children's privacy, I am truly grateful for their willingness to allow their stories to be told in this context. There is a certain danger in revealing the moments in the life of a family when things changed, hearts were broken, and new life began. The scars of adolescence take a long time to heal, and neither my children nor I are very far removed from those traumas. Nevertheless, the stories are true, and the experiences offered all of us a chance to live into the richness of being a family informed by the Gospels.

Because my youngest child is nineteen at the time of this writing, and my oldest is twenty-eight, I know that my stories are part of the past and I am already out of date. Any story I remember must be supplemented by the challenges of a new day and new lessons to be learned. Only recently, I heard about dryer sheets and liter soda bottles being used to control certain smells filling an enclosed space. Exhaling through the dryer sheet and into the bottle keeps your bedroom from smelling like the substance you were smoking. Who thought of that? And only about a month ago did I learn that the daughter of a friend is a ritual cutter—someone who self-inflicts harm by cutting herself. She has been in my house more than a dozen times. I never noticed. I never asked. I never knew, and I am so sorry. So I write this from a particular perspective. Neither clergy, nor scholar, I write from my life experience.

I trust that a meditation will be more broadly useful than a theological treatise. While I do believe that Christians need a better theology of adolescence, and I am doing my best to support that work, what I offer here is a meditation in particularities: my meditation on the one and only story in the Gospels which focuses on the precarious and challenging nature of a holy twelve-year-old and its impact on my own parenting. This meditation has been shaped by my reading of the Scriptures and other faith-based texts over three decades as well as by my own experience as an adolescent and then as the mother of three. In the final chapter, I offer a brief overview of my own theology of adolescence in the hopes that it will fuel discussions and considerations that will in time provide all of us with a working understanding and vocabulary for this holy time of life.

I am deeply indebted to the men and women I have met all across the country over the last ten years. In implementing the Journey to Adulthood curriculum in parishes nationwide, I met hundreds of parents and youth workers: single, married, divorced, straight, gay, young, and not so young anymore. I learned more from them than I can ever say. Some of their stories are tucked into this text, but more are held close to my heart. The honesty with which they were willing to tell me about their own lives and the lives of the young people in their care fueled my willingness to write this book.

A few words of thanks are in order: I wish to thank the Rev. Thomas Midyette for giving me the opportunity to work on a program of adolescent faith formation, which later became the Journey to Adulthood, and for the many hours we spent together, talking, debating, laughing, and praying. Thank you to Elizabeth Tompkins for being a wise friend and mentor. Thank you to my mom and dad, who, among so many other things, taught me to be brave and strong. Thank you, Jennifer, Emily, and Will for making me a mother. Thank you to my friend and confidante, Kevin Hackett SSJE, who together with all the rest of the brothers of the Society of Saint John the Evangelist, cared for me and prayed for me and this book at every step of the way. Every author should be so lucky. Thank you to the hardworking and capable staff of Cowley Publications, especially my editor, Ulrike Guthrie, who read with an open heart and a clear mind. And finally, my deepest thanks to Kirsten for her affectionate listening, for pouring me another cup of coffee, and for reading and re-reading every word.

Amanda Millay Hughes

Adolescence gives all species
a hard time of it, and our own
most of all...The only way
through is the way ahead—
to our adulthood.

Robert Granat

SOMETHING ABOUT ADOLESCENCE challenges adult and adolescent alike. Maybe it's the moodiness or the hysterical laughter. Suddenly there are endless phone calls, secret conversations, and new rules. The bickering, body odor, and a whole new wardrobe are nothing compared to the small smile that stands in for a true kiss goodbye. A shrug of the shoulders and a grunt are all most parents can hope for. Every parent and every child has a personal list. Maybe adolescence is such a challenge because everyone involved has the nagging sense that we are doomed to endure it and unsure how to survive it.

If for no other reason than this, adolescence is hard on everybody: suddenly, by previously unavailable means, teenagers are finding their ways to God, answering or avoiding the invitation God extends to each one to come forward out of childhood, through the tunnel of the teen years, and into the rigors and blessings of adulthood. It is a holy time of life, bringing so much unfamiliar noise and even more peculiar silence into the home. I am getting my last taste of it. If I am lucky, grandchildren will usher it all back to me one more time, but it will be a while yet.

My children are no longer children. All three have made it through the journey of their own adolescence, and while I would be lying if I said it was easy on any of us, the exhilaration and the disappointments surpassed any roller coaster ride. Strapped in by the bonds of our affection and our obligations to one another, holding on for dear life, it's a ride that took my breath away and gave it back to me, put my heart in my throat and made me cry out to God. It also made me laugh, scream, punish, forgive, and more than once, prevented any assurance that God was hearing, much less answering, my many prayers.

Of the three people who call me Momma, Will, my youngest, is nineteen. Emily, the middle child, is twenty-one, and Jennifer, my oldest daughter, is twenty-eight. Jennifer is married, sings in a club band as many as four nights a week, year round, knows all the lyrics to virtually every pop song since 1958, and in her spare time, teaches middle school math and science at a public school in Guilford County, North Carolina. Emily graduated from college a year ahead of schedule, drove herself out Old Route 66—to celebrate its seventy-fifth anniversary—landed in Los Angeles for a summer internship with Egg Pictures, came back home and packed her bags, boxes, and pots and pans and moved up to Brooklyn to study acting at the New Actor's

Workshop. She wanders the Big Apple by way of the metro, slipping her pass through the turnstile every morning and evening as she commutes in and out of Manhattan. Will is a freshman at Appalachian State University. He journeys up and down the mountain with some regularity, driving an old red Mazda pickup truck, with a new CD and stereo unit (he paid for) that cost nearly half what we paid for the truck itself.

I cannot pinpoint the day when I knew they were no longer children any more than I can find a particular moment in my memory when this tender regard for young people and their parents took such powerful root in me. I only know that it has. I know for certain that it began with an uncanny awareness of the consequences of disregard. It was not so much the attention of love that made me aware of the mystery of being a teen, rather it was the pain of love withheld, voices silenced, anger grown palpable. In the moments of greatest challenge, I began to notice that turning away had its own unforeseen consequences. When I let myself remember, I know that these were the moments in which transformation and forgiveness began. The psalmist writes, "The Lord enlarged me when I was in distress" (Psalm 4.1 KJV). Adolescence is a time of distress, and it is a time for enlarging the heart.

I suspect that this tender regard began when I was a teenager. I slammed the door. I turned away. I broke the rules. The most likely memory, the first insight, came after I deeply hurt my mother by calling her a potentially unforgivable name. I can still see the look on her face when I said it. She was shocked, stunned, and hurt. I was indignant, defiant, and caught, like a deer in the headlights. In that moment, I learned something: the frustration and defiance that are the hallmark of adolescence are opportunities for healing and forgiveness. In the moments of deepest hurt and disregard we can turn toward one another and away from shame and consequent remorse. Neither my mother nor I turned away. We looked at each other, tears in both our eyes. I asked her to forgive me. She did and she grounded me for six weeks.

It was during these teenage years of mine—in the 1970s, when it was cool to be both a Christian and a teenager, to ask strangers to be born again, to attend worship meetings and Bible studies in the homes of my equally comfortably middle-class friends, to love Jesus more than anything else, to know the Bible's stories inside and out and memorize verses in the King James Version—it was during these years that I first read Luke's gospel and encountered the Lost-and-Found-Jesus.

> Every year his parents went to Jerusalem for the Feast of the Passover. When he was twelve years old, they went up to the Feast, according to the custom. After the Feast was over, while his parents were returning home, the boy Jesus stayed behind in Jerusalem, but they were unaware of it. Thinking he was in their company, they traveled on for a day. Then they began looking for him among their relatives and friends. When they did not find him, they went back to Jerusalem to look for him. After three days they found him in the Temple courts, sitting among the teachers, listening to them and asking them questions. Everyone who heard him was amazed at his understanding and his answers. When his parents saw him, they were astonished. His mother said to him, "Son, why have you treated us like this? Your father and I have been anxiously searching for you."
>
> "Why were you searching for me?" he asked. "Didn't you know I had to be in my Father's House?" But they did not understand what he was saying to them.
>
> Then he went down to Nazareth with them and was obedient to them. But his mother treasured all these things in her heart. And Jesus grew in wisdom and stature, and in favor with God and men. (Luke 2:41-52 NIV)

As a teenager, it was Jesus' adventure and his challenging questions to his mother that intrigued me. More than thirty years later, it is the concern of his parents that makes my heart ache. There is enough in these twelve verses to contemplate for a lifetime: it is the only story in our Scriptures in which we meet Jesus as an adolescent. It is the first time Jesus speaks in the gospel of Luke. It is a simple story of the lost and found Son of God, and it is a complex invitation to consider how we become who we are as children, as young people, as mothers and fathers, and as elders. It is a story that reminds us of the importance of finding the Lost and Found. And compassion is at the heart of the matter.

Compassion, as I am using the word in this context, is not some touchy-feely sense that we understand another person's experience. It is hardly useful to tell teenagers, "I know what you're going through," as though my experience of adolescence bears much, if any, resemblance to theirs. Compassion isn't a feeling at all. Compassion is action. It expresses itself as participation in the life and passion of another.

Compassion binds families together. The more we act in accordance with the need of the other, even when it is painfully expensive to the self, the greater the likelihood that we will not merely survive adolescence, but learn in it, grow through it, and answer the call of God. So while I would have liked to breeze through my own teenage years and my children's, that is not the path of compassion. I would have liked to understand everything that happened as it happened, but understanding one another is only one small part of what was and is needed. Understanding is limited while compassion knows no end. I needed compassion, and so did my children.

The transition from child to adult is always expensive, costing time, energy, love, devotion, sacrifice, dedication, discipline, obedience, and even passion. Yet spending dollars on new shoes is not nearly as necessary as spending time together in the choosing and trying on. A bigger family room is not nearly as important as a bigger heart. Quality time is essential, but not at the expense of quantity. We must all make sacrifices, but turning away and missing the moments when true transformation is possible must not be part of our sacrifice just because our children are now teenagers and the difficulty appears insurmountable. It is not enough to understand, endure, and survive adolescence. We must all get our hands and our hearts dirty involving ourselves in the process of living it together if we are to fulfill the gospel call to compassion. If we ignore adolescence, we will find ourselves blind to its graces. If we despise it, we will miss so many opportunities for joy. If we say this is the best time in life, we will be lying. God has no need of our lies. Neither do our teenagers.

So I say it again: compassion requires that we act in accordance with the needs of the other, even when it is painfully expensive to the self. Compassion requires that we love without coercion. Give without expectation of return. Seek without any assurance of finding what we seek beyond the assurance Jesus offers when he tells us, "Seek and you will find" (Matthew 7:17). I understand that we might be seeking a relationship with a young person who is, by any and all methods of honest reckoning, making us crazy. But compassion is one way that love is made visible in the world and one way to carve out a path that will unite mother and daughter, father and son, elder and teen in this journey through our lives.

Compassion invites us to allow the superficial to become superfluous, to lead with more than words or even actions but with the deepest wisdom of the heart. When we find ourselves lacking that deepest wisdom, compassion reminds us to seek new information and to place that knowledge within the embrace of our relationships. Knowledge, when combined with the tenderness of real relationships with real people, breeds wisdom. And wisdom will always give birth to both candor and mercy whenever we face up to what is real, listen to the heart of the gospel, and look for the core of our experience. If we are to survive adolescence, if we are to be effective with young people, offering them the truthful, good news of God, we will need to practice candor and mercy, giving to them that which we most desire for ourselves—unbridled compassion.

So when parents ask me how they will survive these years, I say: compassion. This time of life lures all of us into a deeper knowledge of God's call on our lives. Not only does God call our children in new and unexpected ways, but us as well. Adolescence invites parents as well as teens to embrace new opportunities to balance desire with obedience, novelty with responsibility, memory with destiny, and disappointment with hope.

The gospel story of Jesus in the Temple calls us to love one another, even and especially teens, in exactly the way that Mary and Joseph loved Jesus, Jesus loved his parents, the elders loved his questions and his answers, and Jesus loved the attention the elders gave to his concerns. Everyone in the story offers a reminder of the many ways in which God has so compassionately loved us all. Adolescence is a difficult time of life filled with unforeseeable and often unimaginable changes in every aspect of our experience. It is a roller coaster ride filled with agonizing anticipation, heartache and loss as well as mystery and miracle, adventure and sheer delight. Reflecting on the teen years of my children, and looking back on my own journey from childhood to adulthood yields nothing less than a gospel story—filled to the brim with meaning, with metaphor, with mystery and, yes, filled with the powerful presence of God's compassion.

chapter one

The Challenging Child

> The challenge is in
> the balance; to go as near
> to the edge, as near to
> the power and the mystery
> and the danger as possible
> without falling into chaos.
>
> *Sara Maitland*

W HEN MY CHILDREN were growing up, the dinner
table was the place we played a favorite game. It
was a word game, a game of story and
conversation, which began each night when someone
asked, "What was the Best Part of the Day?" Sometimes
willingly, sometimes with great reticence, and sometimes
in angry compliance, each member of the family offered
a story. The only requirement was that it had to be true.
Twists of plot and surprise endings were not uncommon.
Sometimes the stories were light-hearted and very

funny, but of course, sometimes the game led to tears and unanticipated conflicts. We structured our dinner conversation with this question from the time my children were old enough to speak. Because we are a real family, with all the ups and downs that make for a normal life, we conceded to misery on really rotten days and allowed ourselves to tell the truth: there was no best part of the day. Never letting go of the game, we shared the worst part of the day instead. It was our touchstone, one small attempt to stay connected, and every night, good and bad, we came home to ourselves by way of a round robin conversation with one and then another piping in along the way and every one taking a turn.

As in most social groups, a pattern quickly established itself in our conversation. Emily, the middle child, always wanted to go last, at least in part, I suspect, because of her desire for distinction. She was already endlessly in the middle, and her stories were not going to be mundane. She determined to have the best or the worst story of the day and so needed to listen to all the others before she would begin her own. Will, the baby, often wanted to go first. His stories were then as they are now: short, pithy, and straight to the point. Jennifer, the oldest, almost seven years older than Emily, would offer a long and rambling story about her day.

One night, when Jennifer was in the fifth grade, she described the worst part of her day. In preparation for a homework assignment, the math teacher had handed each student a set of geometric shapes cut from black cardboard. The pieces could be put together in any number of ways to form a seemingly endless list of recognizable shapes. The assignment was simple enough: take all the pieces (you had to use them all every time) and arrange them until the shape looked like the required picture on the sheet. Jennifer couldn't do it. After dinner, we tried for over an hour. We pushed back the placemats, let the dinner dishes wait, and tried to turn rectangles, triangles, and parallelograms of black cardboard into a butterfly, a house, and a horse. We failed miserably. Jennifer's frustration mounted, turning into tears. I wrote a short note on the bottom of the homework paper explaining, "We tried and we failed. What are we missing?" and signed my name.

Predictably, the best part of Jennifer's next day came in math class because she did get it. With a little help and encouragement from her teacher, Jennifer continued to spin the pieces and place them in new configurations. The teacher assured Jennifer that as soon as she figured out how to do one, she would quickly get them all. That night after dinner, Jennifer gave the same advice to me, and yes, it worked. We made butterflies and airplanes and chariots.

At Christmas that year, I found a commercially manufactured set of shapes, marketed as *Tangrams*. We played and played with that set of shapes, often laughing over how impossibly hard it had seemed the first night and how fun it had become over time. Endurance was necessary and rewarded.

Constructing One's Own Narrative Life

I suppose I remember this one bad and then good day precisely because they offer such a fine metaphor for the struggle to understand one's own life, particularly as a teenager. Learning to see differently, to see one's experience as greater than the sum of parts, to assemble and then reassemble the given shape of one's experience, is all a part of the struggle to be who we are. Our habitual "Best Part of the Day" game helped my children, and me, to remember the importance of constructing a working narrative out of the day's events. In the telling, we learned to find shape and meaning in our lives.

But for a time there, when they were early adolescents, a marked change occurred in our dinner table ritual. Yes, we still sat down together, and yes, they dutifully told one tale or another, but I could see something across the table that I had not seen before. They delved into their own experience of the world, lived at least a part of every day without their mother's endless presence and prescience. They met new friends and new challenges, and much of it happened without telling me. I knew there were aspects of their stories that they were intentionally keeping from me. Questions of meaning, desire, longing, the deepest joys and laughter were no longer included as readily as I might have hoped. They went through the motions, filled in the most visible gaps but kept a good-sized portion of their inner lives hidden.

Later in the evening, when my children were together in the family room, watching television or working on homework, I might hear them break into uncontrollable giggles with one another. If I came into the room, they would look at me as though I were the champion of an invading army, intending to rob them of their territory. The look in their eyes informed me that I could not possibly understand what was so funny—though to be fair, the few times they tried to explain, I didn't understand, didn't find it funny, and had to admit to myself that I was standing somewhere outside the boundaries of their humor. In many ways, while adolescence is a wild and wonderful time for youth, it is a time of sorrow for parents. I had grown all too accustomed to the company of my children. As they disappeared, reframed, and re-formed themselves into young teenagers, and then into young adults, it was easy to feel that I had been left somewhere in the middle distance, watching from a remote vantage. To some extent, the view was and remains tinged with sorrow and loneliness. It is so natural to feel that something terrible has happened, to determine that something must have gone wrong.

Having lost some of the easy connection I had long felt with my children, my first instinct was to call them back. Now. Right away. Immediately. I wanted to probe them with questions, grill them for details. I pondered the moral implications of breaking into their diaries, reading their e-mail, talking to their teachers or calling the mothers of their friends. One time, I considered cornering them in the car on the drive to school one time and, with my finger set on the automatic door locks, saying, "Okay, tell me everything. Right here, right now." I wanted to buckle each one of them back into infant car seats and refuse to let them out until they told me everything. This unnamed feeling that welled up cursed me with moments of rage and disappointment and confusion. It turned me into my own mother—not that this is necessarily a bad thing, it just came as a big surprise. If I could have wrapped words around this unnamed feeling, the words might have sounded like this: "Please, don't go."

But children have to go.

I have often wondered of all the stories that the writers of the Gospels might have included in their narrative of Jesus' life, why did only Luke choose to include one story—and only one—from his childhood, one in which he has an adventure away from his parents. At least at first reading, it seems something went terribly wrong. Over the last decade, I have come to believe that nothing went wrong in Jesus' family, and nothing had gone wrong in mine. Nothing was wrong in the family next door either. In fact, things were going wonderfully right. My own children were moving away from me, becoming people I barely knew in order that they might become the people that they were meant to be by God's grace and design.

My children might not have agreed with me had I said this to them in the midst of their adolescence, but I believe that young people disappear from view and create these complex social webs and secret agendas in order to check out whether everything we taught them in childhood is really and honestly true. It is as if they must take time away from us—perhaps physically, certainly psychically—in order to see who they are, what the world looks like, and whether we, as parents and adults who work with children, have been telling them the truth. Are our views reliable? Will they really need all the things that we have insisted are essential and instilled in their lives? Is the gospel true? Is the individual gospel of our lives, the one we taught (and they memorized) in everything we have ever said, done, or remembered aloud in their presence, is it all true?

This is one of the hardest pressures a parent can face. The very nature of our truth is called into question. We are forced to defend the way we live our lives at the very same time that we are expected to rearrange our routines to accommodate changes in our children's sleep patterns, the surge of hormones in the household, increased activities, club memberships, and mountainous school work. It doesn't help that these challenges often coincide with our own mid-life crises. Any one of these demands would be more than enough, but living with a teenager means they all come into the household with concomitant fervor. The whole process can seem unnecessary and annoying. Is it any wonder that so many households in which teenagers live are filled with stress and strain?

Testing the Truth

In response to exactly one stressed parent's plea, I called a psychotherapist friend of mine for a referral. In a thousand different ways the parents said, "She's messed up. She is lost. She needs help." When I called him, he declined to see the girl unless the whole family came with her. "Usually, when a teenager is in crisis, the whole family is in crisis," he said, and went on, "The problems didn't originate with the child. The acting out is about challenging the truth in the family."

Teenagers are in the business of challenging truth. Given the fact that teens are often not terribly skillful at framing the challenge, and given that we may not understand the nature of their dilemmas, let alone our own, it is not surprising that teen years are times of turmoil within family systems.

So often in our conversations about teens, we misunderstand this challenge of truth as a general challenge of authority. Growing through my teen years, my own mother often said, "Don't test me." It never occurred to me that I was testing her, and her announcing that I was only engendered rage. Even my rage defied articulation. Now I can look back and recognize that I was not testing her, at least not directly. I was testing the truth, one truth against another, her truth against mine. This is not to say that teens never challenge authority. They do. I know I did. They push the boundaries. Because they know us so well, they press our buttons handily. But they are doing it for at least one good reason: they need to find out if what we have said is true. The truth I am talking about does not submit itself to formulas and equations. It is relational, discovered in the space created between us, the stories we have lived through. The truth binds us together, and sometimes it tears families apart.

Everything we have taught our children about the church and the world, family and faith, politics and pastries, all of it comes up for challenge at just about the same time that puberty sets in. Hormones fuel not only new affections, but new questions, new insights, and new demands. Everything we have ever said about friend and foe is being scrutinized and compared to their own experience. Our children compare our dinner table wisdom with the wisdom of their peers. They watch the television to see if their lives and their families measure up. Even when it appears that they are not listening or paying us the slightest regard, they watch to see if we actually do pray during the prayers in Sunday services and what possible impact that may have on how we face the world by Tuesday morning. They wonder if God is as good, as great, as powerful, and as merciful as all the songs and psalms and sermons promise. Even when it appears they are sleeping, they hear every word spoken in their homes. They are the keepers of secrets. They ask the right questions for the right reason: they need to know what is true. From what jokes we find funny to what sorrows we find unbearable, from what gasoline we buy to what we believe about sex, drugs, and rock and roll, all of it is challenged in early and mid adolescence.

What makes this particularly difficult is that on a conscious level, most teenagers are unaware of their search. Imagine the *Tangrams* spread across the table. In a steady stream of wondering, and testing and trying, retreating and coming around again to start the examination one more time, every shape of our lives is shuffled. The teen drags behind, stands and wonders, stares off into the distance. It is exhausting for the young person and frustrating, if not down right terrifying, for the adult. It is also necessary for the child and necessary for the parent.

Perhaps this is why the story of the lost Jesus is so poignant. He, too, having spent twelve years in the company of his family, suddenly disappears. He stayed behind in Jerusalem. He scoots away into the crowd. Why? First and foremost, because he has to. He must grow up. Children cannot stay children forever. The anatomy and physiology of normal human development pushes us out of the comfort and security of our families and into the grand arena of life and history. Jesus disappeared from sight. Jesus got himself lost in order to challenge the truth of his tradition, his family, and his own sense of himself.

In order for us to grow up, we, too, will have to challenge the status quo that permeated our childhood, the rhythm of our parents' lives, the assumptions under which we developed. We are not meant to remain in the realm of our childhood. Human beings are not designed to be hot house plants who must stay within the shelter of a greenhouse in order to grow and bear fruit. Instead, we are meant to be planted in the rich soil of a broader world, to bear up under fair and foul conditions. Even though, as a parent, twelve or thirteen years old feels far too young for this breakaway, it is developmentally necessary.

Making Our Family Customs Our Own

The story of the lost Jesus recorded in Luke's gospel offers a lovely little hint into the nature of this mysterious and necessary challenge. It tells us that Jesus went with his father and mother to Jerusalem to celebrate the Passover, as was the custom. Rules of proximity in grammar tell the reader that this use of "the custom," following so closely after "his father and mother," may be taken to mean that it is literally *their* custom: Mom and Dad's routine, the normal thing, normal people do for Passover. Yes, Jesus is included in the journey, participates in the celebration, but it is not yet his custom. It is theirs. The tension of the story sits in his struggle to transform the custom into his custom. Jesus needs to internalize the Passover, allowing it to stand as a part of his personal history. To do that, he had to act it out.

It is noteworthy that this story is set in the context of another more ancient one. Passover is the Jewish commemoration of the first steps of the exodus, of the flight from bondage to freedom and the struggle through which the descendents of Abraham made their way from captivity in Egypt, through the Wilderness of Sinai toward the Promised Land. In ritual celebrations, Jewish people to this day remember this passage with great devotion. The celebration includes the telling and retelling of the actions of God in history. It is an annual time of instruction for the young and remembrance for the old. Within the context of instruction and remembrance, Jesus makes his own escape, his own exodus into the world of his own faith.

The Scriptures tell us that he tarried in Jerusalem. He stayed behind. He disappeared. It is not difficult to imagine how this might have happened. Mary and Joseph would have traveled with their family members and friends into the Holy City. They would not have come alone. Undoubtedly, Mary and Joseph taught Jesus in the early years of his life to pay attention, show respect, and mind his manners. Upon arrival, they would have seen again the wall that surrounds the city, and they would have recognized the protection it offered to them. I can almost hear Mary speaking to Jesus. She sounds like me. "Go on," she might have said. "Enjoy yourself. See the sights and try the foods, and stay inside the wall." She would have had extra confidence in him for two other reasons: first, he had been there before and second, he was not alone in the city. Because Passover is an annual celebration, and Luke tells us that it was the custom to travel to the city, we can infer that Jesus had been to Jerusalem every year of his young life. This was at least his twelfth visit to the Holy City. He knew his way around its tangled web of streets. He knew where the gates were and the hidden alleyways. He would be fine. He should not be a bother to anyone. They would have walked these same streets together many, many times. If that were not enough to let him loose in the city, maybe the fact that all their friends and relatives were there was assurance as well. People watched out for one another. Surely they would see Jesus at the vendors' tables. Certainly, they would walk with him a little distance here, and hand him off to another adult acquaintance there. Even if he happened to slip away for a few minutes, the city itself was small. How far could he go? How much trouble could he possibly get into during the days surrounding the celebration?

Then comes the challenge. Jesus stays behind. He disappears from view. He breaks the rule. For Jesus and for us, challenging the truth is not a negative action; it is a necessary one. Jesus actively challenged the protection of his family and the truths they had taught him by disappearing from under the umbrella of his family's most immediate and necessary concern. He went looking. He walked this way and that.

Did he look carefully in each vendor's stall? Did he whistle and run? Did he lean against the walls and watch as families with younger children passed him on their way? No matter where I imagine him, he is not lost. He is in familiar territory. He knows the city. The story is not set in the vast wilderness that surrounds Jerusalem, but in Jerusalem proper.

The Incremental Exodus

I would never advocate for the application of this story into the wide wilderness of our own culture. Teenagers should not make their first exodus into completely unfamiliar territory. It must happen within the boundaries of a wider community, and within the context of the family's customs. Jesus is lost in a city that his parents know very well, during the celebration of a well-known and beloved time of holy remembrance. He is lost in the context of his community and also in the context of his stream of faith history. In other words, Jesus is moving into the wider framework of his own story, but he is not moving into the world at large. The exodus that young people can rightly take from their families must be incremental: from the house to the neighborhood, from the neighborhood to the school, from the school to the community, from my life into their own. It is ever widening, but it must be taken step by step.

This incremental motion from inside to outside, from here to there, is essential for all young people if they are to move safely from childhood to adulthood. The passage is difficult. It is not easy to be born. As every mother knows—it is a bloody and difficult task, filled with pushing and pulling and pain. Difficulty rarely negates necessity and almost always accompanies it.

The same can be said about the transition from inside the family, from inside parental concerns to the concerns of a broader sensibility. It is a difficult task, filled with pushing and pulling and pain. Children find new and secret passageways across the yard and under the fence to arrive at their friends' homes. We may forbid it, reminding them to walk the way we have always walked, around the block and on the sidewalk, but the new path has been established. It is their own. Teenagers are charting the same kind of passageways. There will be scuffed knees and bruised egos along the way, but a new passageway will be discovered. It may be helpful to think of this whole process as a kind of map making. We have charted a certain path within our own map of the world and our children reject it, determined not only to find their own, but to create the big picture that only such explorations can afford them. They are making a new map of the world as they know it. One path at a time. Like birth itself, this is a necessary struggle.

Life-giving Rules

If this change is so necessary and right, why does it cause enormous conflict in some families, while in others almost none? Why do some families barely notice the transition and others fixate on it? There may be as many reasons as there are families, and as many ways to make this change as there are reasons. One thing is certain, there must be true customs in the lives of the adults in a family in order for the child to break away.

Years ago, in a youth group setting, I asked the young people to make a list of all the rules in their households. Generally, the rules have to do with curfew—what time you must be in; household chores—who is going to clean the bathroom, and how often; and entertainment—what movies, videos and music are acceptable. But this time, and several times in subsequent years, a member of the group sat silent and still through the whole exercise and most of the discussion. When I became aware of the boy's reticence, I asked him, "What rules do you have in your house?" He answered, "None." Then a moment later added, "I guess the only rule is that there are no rules. We just do our own thing."

I worry about families in which there are no rules and no customs. It looks too much like a house full of individuals, but no family; bloodlines, but no ties that bind. It is hard to be a family without certain expectations and behaviors that bind us together. Every family needs its own creed, a kind of heart beat that reminds all the members of what they believe, hope for, and long for. There needs to be an assurance of identity that every member of the family understands and can employ as they establish the rhythm of their lives. If there is no creed, then the challenging of the truth that young people have to make is threatened. There must be something strong enough to bear the pull of our young people. The family must be strong enough to give the pull away a little tug in return.

Giving Pull

Several years ago, I decided I would learn how to square dance. I found a group that met in a local elementary school gymnasium and at which both beginners and experts were welcome. In the half hour before the official start time, the experts offered basic instructions. As the time for the dancing approached, people poured into the gym, some dressed in street clothes, others in traditional dancing outfits. The music began and we were off.

I am not good at this organized dancing. I struggle to coordinate my body with the beat and the movements. But one night, after about an hour and a half, I was beginning to think I was getting the hang of it. I didn't feel lost and I hadn't embarrassed myself. We were moving around the enormous circle in what I remember as a "grand right and left," when all of a sudden we were to spin with the next partner. We were supposed to cross our arms and grab hold of the forearm of the next partner, and spin. I thought I had done exactly the right thing, but my partner was not pleased. "Give pull," he said against the music. "Give what?" I called back. "Give pull," and he was off to the next steps in the dance. I had no idea what he meant. At the end of the evening, he came across the room to me. He said, "In a spin, you have to give pull." I told him that I didn't know what he meant. He grabbed my arms and started to spin around again. He said, "Now pull! Pull away from me and I will pull away from you. We're going to hold on, but we are also going to pull away. The caller will tell us when to let go."

It is not a bad analogy for raising and working with adolescents. Adults have to give pull. There must be expectations. The traditions and customs in our families give pull to our young people and keep them from flying off. When we hold on with a tight enough grasp to let them lean away, hold on as they spin through the adolescent years, in a very real sense, through the grip of hand to forearm, we can give our children the energy and momentum necessary to break away. If we hold on too loosely and refuse to pull, then they will not be ready for the next steps in the dance. If we don't hold on tight enough, they will not learn the true power of relationships. We have to hold on, and they have to pull away. We are a family after all. This is not a dormitory. There has to be a push and a pull if there is to be transformation.

Letting Go Is Unacceptable

The opposite danger lies in having too tight a grasp. In the same youth group there was a young person who said, "There are so many rules in my house, I don't even know which ones really matter." Her list was exceedingly long. Young people, like adults, need to know what really matters. Is it the same level of infraction to leave your shoes on the couch as it is to leave the house without writing a note? Why? Don't some things matter more than others? Families, like individuals, need a hierarchy of meaning, a way of organizing the demands and the restrictions of a common life. If too many rules restrict the motion and understanding of the teen, they will break away in anger, with bruises on their arms. They may leave the family dance altogether, and often, too soon.

But there is yet another possible cause of the chaos and anger, or total disengagement in families during the teen years. I have often heard parents say that they made so many mistakes in raising their children when they were little that by the time adolescence arrives, they just give up. As one mother said, "We have been fighting with each other since my daughter was five. I am exhausted. I give up." I know what it's like to feel certain that you have made so many mistakes along the way that there is no chance your children will grow up normal, let alone well-adjusted and faith-filled. Still, I always tell them the same thing, the same thing I told myself in the midst of my own children's teen years: don't give up.

I am completely convinced that completely letting go of a son or daughter while they are still living in our households is an *unacceptable option*. If we do, we will have turned them into the stranger, released them from the reality of the family's life. They will become outsiders, witnesses to the life of the family, but no longer full participants in it.

At that same dance night, I watched several young teens sit on the sidelines as their parents danced. At first they were willing to watch, tap their feet, and pay attention. But an hour later, they were gone, huddled outside with their peers. I remember overhearing one father as he went looking for the daughter he had lost. She was not in the huddle by the back door. If we don't give pull, holding on to our young people, there are innumerable places for them to turn to find someone who will.

Holding On Whatever The Cost

What can be done even when it seems like it is too late? Establish a simple set of customs. Make a habit of asking, *What was the best part of your day?* Turn off the television. Don't answer the phone for a few minutes. Give a little pull. It's never too late for that. And as for teens, when they tell me that their parents are driving them away, making them crazy, ignoring them, or picking fights, I try to tell them the truth. Adolescence is hard on everybody...the lost and the found. When I imagine Mary and Joseph searching frantically for Jesus, up and down the narrow streets, calling his name, looking and looking again, not knowing that Jesus could be found seated with the elders in the Temple, I have to wonder who was truly lost in the story? The boy or his parents?

The model of Jesus and his challenge of truth is a model for all of us. If we fail to do the work of challenging the truth as teens, we will do it as young adults, or worse, as a part of a protracted midlife crisis. It is essential that we slip away into the wider circle of our customs to see if and why they are true. The Bible teaches that much of what Jesus found when he examined the history of the faith and the history of his own family, he ultimately redefined. It happens time and again in the gospels when Jesus says, "You have heard it said...but I say to you..." That is a good thing. It should not surprise us, as adults, or terrify us that there is the chance that our youth will reject some and redefine much of what we have taught them. This, too, is an essential part of growing up. Part of living an adult life is taking responsibility for the truth. Jesus did it. So will our children as they move from childhood to adulthood.

Will they disappear from view? Yes. It is wrong? No. It is necessary.

chapter two

The Problem of Identity

...and my windows
might be dirty
but it's my house
and if I can't
see out sometimes
they can't see in either.

Nikki Giovanni

PARENTS OFTEN WONDER ALOUD, "Who is this kid?"
Though rhetorical, the question is also very wise.
The child they have loved and taken care of for
years has become someone they no longer know and
understand. This is not surprising when we recall that
young people are actively engaged in what developmental
psychologists might call "creation of the self." Plagued by
an imaginary audience which critiques every thought,
burdened by a body experiencing more dramatic change
than at any other time in life, while haunted and perhaps

even hounded by the expectations of friends, family, and faith, an adolescent searches for opportunities which might both define and reveal his or her identity. For the most part, this search happens in the private territory of the inner life, in a room without windows. We cannot see in, but they cannot see out either. We may or may not see a change in clothing style, hair color, friends, interests, and manners. But whether by a change of appearance, or by spending time with the elders in Jerusalem, one way or another, teens will distance themselves from the captivity of their childhood to experience the wilderness, where anything and everything is possible.

I have often wondered which would have been worse for Jesus when he was a child: to know who he was or to have no idea. This must be one of the mysteries of the Incarnation. Did Jesus know who he was, fully, completely, even when he was little? Wouldn't that have been an unbearable burden? On the other hand, if he had to discover it, then certainly that, too, would have been at least momentarily horrifying. At what point in anyone's life is one's full destiny truly bearable? It seems to me that Jesus must have known and that he could not have fully known. He must have felt something in his heart that was as unique to him, as he was unique in history. Perhaps he knew just that much even when he was too young to speak. But, he also must have discovered the fuller meaning and its true significance a little at a time. Either way, there were certainly times when Jesus had to face down the demands of his true self and struggle to come to terms with what he knew and what he did not know of the consequences.

I believe that if Jesus had a hard time figuring out not only who he was, but how to be the unique child of God, then surely all of our children are in for a comparable struggle.

The Struggle for Self-Understanding

Despite the many advances in our knowledge, we still know relatively little about the brain. Experts in development and psychology tell us that when a young person reaches the age of thirteen or fourteen, something incredible and mysterious begins to happen. Neural pathways all but explode with activity. Even while they are sleeping, adolescents continually search for the most efficient way to think. Teenagers uncontrollably think and think and think until they can arrive at the fastest path from question to answer, logic to reason, from love to action, from "two plus two" to logarithms. No wonder they are so tired.

At the same time, they are able to do a type of thinking that they have never done before. They can imagine and conceptualize ideals. I remember writing a paper in the ninth grade in which I argued that the ideal government would be a benevolent dictatorship—as long as the dictator never died. Sounds a bit like heaven to me, now. Today my ideal government is more closely akin to membership within the Body of Christ than the Democratic Party. Teenagers can imagine ideal communities. An ideal God. An ideal family. No wonder they bicker with reality with such ferocity and passion. No wonder they are cross with everybody. No wonder they don't like us. We hardly ever live up to our own ideals, let alone an adolescent image of the ideal human, who probably lives in a family that looks more like *The Brady Bunch* with a clean house and deafening communal intent, than an episode of *Roseanne*, where chaos is almost unrestrained. Yet I have heard a teenager perplexed by *The Brady Bunch*, saying, "If God were really as loving and kind as everybody says, then the original mother and father in *The Brady Bunch* would never have died in the first place." The idealism applies to television and movies and to rules in chess, soccer, and the rankings in the ACC. It also applies to the self. For the first time in their lives, teenagers are capable of imagining their ideal selves.

The ideal self is stronger, kinder, thinner, taller, smarter, older, braver, funnier, cooler, sexier, wiser, more forgiving, more dedicated, more compassionate, more brilliant, more productive, more honest, a little gentler, a lot fiercer, well-dressed, and rich. The ideal self is so right that it can be unyielding, but not without being very good at meaningful compromise. The ideal self can get up in the morning without a mother knocking at the door or an alarm clock bleeping into the dark.

My daughter Emily says that she can remember looking at a particular image of Cindy Crawford in a red dress: rich, tall, and voluptuous. She says she knew that was never going to be her. She also says that because she was smart in middle school—the mightiest curse for so many young girls who long for a fun social life—she determined to reject that idealism. She decided to identify the ideal, reject it, and then determined that her ideal self was self-determining. Now, at twenty, still brilliant, but also something of a rival to Cindy Crawford's beauty, once again, she has to self-determine what it means to be Emily. It is a very difficult struggle indeed.

Or take another example. When Will was born, he came into the world with rather large ears. Now there are cultures in the world where this would be considered a grace, but America in the 1980s was not one of them. To make matters worse, when he was eleven or twelve, he was short, stocky, and got the worst hair cut any boy of twelve could ever imagine. His ears were reminiscent of Dumbo—and he knew it. What did he do? He determined he would never cut his hair again. For the next six years, Will let his hair grow until it was all the way down his back. Why? Because his ideal self demanded it. He grew almost ten inches in height without gaining any weight the same year that he decided to let his hair grow. He transformed himself into the King of Cool.

Years later, Will told me that the number one thing he learned in high school was to be himself. He said he wanted to be the most popular kid in the school, and he said he learned there was only one way to make that happen: be who you are. At fifteen, when he entered high school, his ideal self was popular. He tried on a lot of different personas in his search for the ideal self. He changed his name to Felix for a while. He changed his circle of friends several times. He never showed anyone his chest for years.

Living up to Expectations

It is not easy to be aware of the ideal and stuck in your God-given body. At least for most of us. Even for those young people that seem to have been blessed with perfect skin and a metabolism that allows them to eat everything in sight and still arrive at the perfect weight on the doctor's scale, they too have ideals that they hold out for themselves.

On a trip to the Midwest several years ago, I met a sixteen-year-old, the daughter of clergy, who was studying for the SAT. She had made note cards of every word in the SAT study guide, and the words were taped up all over the kitchen, the bathroom, and the back hallway in her parent's home. She was a beautiful, well-dressed, well-spoken young woman. Her parents left the room for a few minutes to freshen up before taking me out to dinner. I asked the girl what score she hoped for on the SAT. She said, "Ideally..." There was that nasty word. She paused and then continued, looking at me and then looking around the kitchen at the hundreds of words. "Ideally, I would score a 1600. That's what I want to do." We talked about her class load—three advanced placement classes for which she would receive college credit if she scored well enough on the tests. We talked about her goals. "Harvard. Princeton, maybe. My dad's people all went to Yale. So Yale, I guess." I listened carefully to what she was saying. There was a pause. And then I said, "You must be very tired." Immediately, she looked at me. Her eyes filled with tears and she said, "They have no idea, you know. No idea how hard it is to be this good."

I told her that I knew. "Being the best little girl in the world is a bitch." She laughed and said, "You got that right. And bitch is not an SAT word." Her parents came in. She stood up. Got a glass of orange juice. Kissed both her mother and father on the cheek, said, "Have fun tonight. You deserve it," and disappeared into the hallway that led up to her room.

I have never met a young person who did not, to one degree or another, struggle to live up to the ideals that suddenly appeared in their consciousness at just about the same time that estrogen and testosterone levels increased. Racked with all this idealism, very little of every day life lives up to the imagined expectations.

The Chatter of the Imaginary Audience

As if that weren't enough, there is still more. Young people also have what the experts call an imaginary audience. They live with an endless audience of well- and ill-meaning sprites, whisperers, critics, and cheerleaders. None of them are actually in the room with them, but like little gnats that circle round your head in the hottest days of July, this Grecian chorus chants out unbridled jibes, critiques, praise, and adulation. It is an endless stream of unconscious thought. I remember one time in particular while shopping for new shoes with Will, when he said, "I can't buy those shoes. I'd be a poser."

"But, do you like them?"

"Yeah, a lot, but Steve has those shoes."

I never met Steve, but his voice had joined the chorus of the imaginary audience.

Why do teenagers look in the mirror and turn up the music and slam the door shut? To silence the imaginary audience. Even unbridled praise can wear you out. Why do they look like they're listening, but then can't remember a word we've said? Because at the very moment we are speaking, so much else is going on inside. The imaginary audience is whispering. The brain is looking for the most efficient way to filter out the noise. The ideal world asks if what we are saying right here, right now, matters all that much anyway? The answer? Probably not.

Now, add in the burden of knowing, deep in your heart, at the core of your being that your life really does matter. Add the sense that you are here for a reason. Add the assurance that you are made in the image of God. Is it any wonder that our teenagers feel lost? Get lost? Lag behind in search of meaning, miracle, and mystery? Lift every rock to see what is hidden underneath it? Or hide in their rooms afraid to come out?

I try to imagine Jesus in the city of Jerusalem. I listen for all the inner voices. Later in the gospels Jesus will confront the devil and demons head on, and so will my children, later in their gospel stories, but at twelve, all Jesus might have been able to do is wander. Look. Listen. Watch. Pay attention.

No Way Back

Most young people know that no matter how much they may want to return to childhood—they cannot. They cannot go back to a time when there were no inner voices and the worst thing in the world was a sad parent. They cannot go back to a small bed, to swift and easy sleep, early rising, and endless running. They know it.

There must have been a moment when Jesus knew that his family had left the city. He must have had at least a passing thought about running after them, finding them, falling into the arms of his mother, letting his eyes fill with tears while wishing she might carry him home. But at twelve, there is no turning back.

While our children may long to return to their childhood, it is no longer available to them. Like the children of Israel passing through the Red Sea as if on dry land, so, too, our children move through an opened passageway and then it closes behind them. There can be no returning to childhood, any more than the children of Israel could pass back through the Red Sea to Egypt. As much as they wanted freedom from bondage, so do our children. As much as they griped and moaned about having had a better life in captivity, our teenagers sometimes long for the restrictions of childhood. They may not admit it, but I believe it is true. As parents, our job is to be sure that we are there on the other side of the Red Sea, singing, like Miriam, about the blessings of being free.

Holding Out the Satisfactions of Adult Life

Funny though, that's not what we do. Most of our discourse with young people about the quality of adult life is tainted with fear, regret and worry. We do not hold out the promised land of one's own life to kids. I remember talking with a group of kids in Oklahoma City a few years before the bombing of the federal office building. A boy of about fifteen, seated in the front row, asked "Why would I want to grow up? All adults do is work too hard, worry too much, and criticize everything." I told him that I know a lot of adults that feel that way—but not all of them. And I did my best to tell him why adulthood is better.

I told him what has been true for me. Because I know how to work at it a little better than I did when I was fifteen, my friends are truer now. We stick by one another in good times and bad. And my parties are better. The boy rolled his eyes. "No really," I said. "I know how to cook now, and I can afford wine bottles with corks." He laughed. But I also told him the truth about the rest. "My love is deeper; the sex is better; my house is mine. I can give money to help the poor, I can choose where and when and how to serve. I can choose to leave, and I can choose to stay. I can choose to go back to school or not."

I honestly believe that one of the greatest gifts we can give our teens is a love for our own lives.

My stepmother died a little over ten years ago, swiftly and suddenly from stomach cancer. It was little more than six weeks from diagnosis to death's door. On one of the last days she was truly lucid, she called me to her, reached for me and asked me to lie down on her bed beside her. I did. I tucked my head up under her shoulder. She had grown very small and frail. She was only sixty-two when she died, and this is among the last things she said to me. She said, "Amanda, it has been a wonderful ride. I have loved every minute of it." I didn't answer. She continued to speak for just a moment more before falling into a restless sleep, "Do what you want to do, Amanda. It's your life."

Helping Teenagers through the Transition

So how can that be made real in the lives of our teenagers? How was it made real for Jesus?

First, we must stay in relationship with our young people, forever working on new strategies for reaching them. Second, we must continue to love our lives while they are struggling to find and create their own.

I say that we must stay in relationship with them because I know of only two things that can silence the imaginary audience and slow the tide of idealism: rock-and-roll music at an ear-piercing volume and true relationships with true people. Since I didn't want to live in a household where music relentlessly pounds from the stereo, I decided on relationship. What I mean by this is complicated and resists handy definition. I mean that we must move toward our kids. Talk to them. Tell the truth. Speak openly about our concerns. Give them tons of opportunity to be who they are. Will changed his name at school, but the first time I called him Felix at home, he said, "Nah, Mom, don't do that. You're ruining it. I am always Will to you." Give them plenty of reason to talk to you. Practice your poker face. Don't be easily shocked. Earnest mothers need to remember how to be silly. Stoic fathers ought to let themselves cry. Learn to feel in the presence of your children. Do not shield them from who you are. Allow your teenager to see and know that you feel emotions beyond fatigue and anger. Set aside time for your teenager, when they are ten, eleven, and twelve. Go out to breakfast every Saturday morning. Take a walk every Wednesday night. Make a ritual. It doesn't take much; it just takes being real. We have to be who we really are in front of them if they are ever going to be who they are in front of us. If we fake it, they will fake it. If we are bored, they will be bored. If we tell the truth and laugh at how hard it is to live into the truth, then they will laugh with us.

The second necessary gift we can give our teenagers is a life we love of which they are a part. Not the center, mind you, but a fabulous part of our lives. I don't think it matters if you are rich or poor, a member of the golf club or if the only membership card you have lets you rent a video, you can let your young person know that they are a part of the richness of your life—and you love them—and you love your life.

Teenagers need to know they are not the center of their parents' lives. Adults should have adults for confidantes and companions. My experience tells me that when teenagers become the center of an adult's life, something is wrong. As often as not, there is no room for the young person to do what must be done—change. If the child is at the center, they are expected to hold the system together by their presence. When they disappear—and they invariably will—the family will falter. When they change, the family will reel. Better for adults to build lives in which their children are a significant, defining, and important focus of love and attention, devotion and grace, but not the center.

Giving Our Children Space to Struggle with the Creation of Self

This is precisely the kind of family Mary and Joseph must have provided for the Son of God, or they never would have let him out of their sight. They were not bad parents because Jesus ended up sitting in the Temple. They were not bad parents because they were able to travel a whole day's journey away from him before they even noticed that he was gone. This is a piece of what made them such good parents. They had their own life, their own circle of friends. Whatever happened to distract them from his whereabouts for a day, ought to remind us to love other people, to be so engaged in our own journeys once in a while that we are, in fact, distracted for a day from the demands of being a full-time dad, a day-in-day-out mom.

As we engage the richness of our own adult lives, we make it possible for our young people to encounter something, Some One, greater than all our limitations and best intentions. In the midst of all the voices young people hear, both real and imaginary, the true voice of God speaks and calls to them. The reality of God presses through the ideals to engage them in what I can only call "the real." The very capacity to imagine ideals widens the possibility of being engaged by the One True Real in all the universe, the ultimate ideal: God. By allowing our teens the time and space to struggle with the "creation of the self," we open the door for a new revelation of who they actually are: beloved children of a loving God. This revelation comes not only to them, but to us as well. If we remain so closely linked to every experience of our children's lives as they move into their teenage years, we radically diminish the possibility of any of us coming to this central truth: my child is God's child. We may have known it when they were small, but we have forgotten. They may have known it when they were little, but they, too, have forgotten, and in unfailing mercy, again God calls to them and to us.

Pay Attention to What is Real

I want to be very clear here and make essential allowances for the many young people who are burdened with mental illnesses and profound issues of self-image and self-loathing. I am not advocating ignoring the sounds that might come out of a corner bathroom. You may well be hearing your daughter vomiting into the toilet after every meal. I am not saying you should be too busy with your own life to notice that your child is hearing voices—not imagining them, but hearing them. I am not saying God is a cure-all for every ill. We all need to pay very close attention, to stay in relationship with our young people as they struggle to discover the truth about themselves, the world, and God. We must break the tacit vow of silence when we see warning signs in our sons and daughters. We must not send them off alone to get fixed by some stranger, but rather, while holding on, join them in therapeutic processes that offer potential aid in healing the whole family.

Even in the most dire times and circumstance, it may be helpful to continue to tell childhood stories while they pass through the Red Sea. Cover the dining room table with baby pictures on their sixteenth birthday. In every way you can imagine, keep alive the richness of their journey. Remember this whole story of Jesus takes place during and immediately following the celebration of the Passover. In the midst of God's deliverance, there were more than a few locusts and plagues. The staff could turn into a wild snake. They made it to the other side of the Red Sea, but not without immeasurable trauma. By actively paying attention to the present and changing realities of our young people's lives, by staying awake to what is going on in our own homes, by telling and retelling the stories of their childhoods, by refusing to rely on empty rhetoric, by telling our tales with laughter, tears, and surprise endings, we can "give pull," as they pull away. Perhaps more important still, we can share in the discovery of who they will become, who they really are.

Every time I thought I finally knew my teenagers again, something would change. Every time I thought I understood what pressures they faced, new pressures appeared and old ones vanished. Adolescence is a time of discovery for them, to be sure, but it is also a time of discovery for us.

Whenever you wonder aloud, "Who is this kid?" remember this: the first, best answer is a beloved child of a loving God.

Work from that truth. Pay attention. Listen closely. Tell the truth. Participate with God in loving them deeply.

chapter three

The Community and the Culture

Unless Christians
become unhurried
and unharried enough
to enjoy a long loving look
at the real, then
Christianity has failed.

William McNamara, OCD

I N THE GOSPEL STORY, Mary and Joseph assume that
their community is supporting and caring for their
son. They have not relinquished responsibility in this
assumption, but rather recognize the necessity of certain
partnerships with friends and family in order to ensure
his safety and his proper upbringing.

It is the very kind of partnership that supports most of
us in our parenting. Mary and Joseph trust that when
they cannot see Jesus, others will watch out for his well-
being, not only in the face of a potentially dangerous

culture, but in the face of the tremendous risks associated with simply growing up. This assumption works well enough, until they realize that Jesus is missing. Once they become aware that Jesus is not, in fact, within the company of friends and family, they are left with a single option: they must search for him.

It is a remarkably human moment in the gospel, reminiscent of so many moments in the lives of moms and dads and youth leaders, teachers and friends. The young person is seen and then suddenly gone. Right next to us, and then, not. It seems as though built into the struggle to offer young people opportunity, we invariably offer them danger as well. The teen years are filled with moments when we are most likely to awaken to our own lives, our own potential, and even our own destiny, that rare combination of the heart's drive and the call of God, and these very same moments are fraught with unpredictable consequences and unforeseen dangers.

Allowing Freedom Amidst Control

As a mom, I know that love compelled me to balance my need for control with my children's needs for freedom. It is a terrifying mix and a delicate balance. From crossing the street for the first time, to climbing onto the school bus, from the first trip away over night to the trip across the continent, and then across the ocean, each of my children has made their own series of sojourns away from me. For the most part, I have felt that I was allowing this motion. In fact, I have often felt that I designed it for them, with carefully demarcated edges and expectations. My expectations extended not only to my children's behavior, but also to the friends and allies I had in their raising. I expected the church to provide certain aspects of religious training, and enough chaperones to keep all young people under a watchful eye. I also expected that my neighbors would silently and with sly focus keep an eye on the house, on the yard, and yes, even on the needs of my children. I expected the medical profession to speak to and inoculate my children against the scariest possibilities of disease. I expected their grandparents to be models of endurance and wisdom.

So it comes as no surprise to me that Mary and Joseph did likewise in the time and place in which they lived and struggled to be good parents. Seeing in the eye of their son a growing interest in the world at large, and acknowledging his own relationships with friends and extended family, it is predictable that they would have allowed him ever expanding freedom. But, freedom has within it enormous risk, even when that freedom has been carefully crafted as more or less an exercise rather than a reality. To put it bluntly, Mary and Joseph lost the Son of God within the labyrinth of their own expectations and assumptions.

I have known moments when I, too, have lost the children of God. Despite my watchfulness, I still had to search for William in Wal-Mart for more than an hour. He had hunkered down in the electronics section to play a new video game. At eight years old, he was far more focused on the moving enemy on the screen than any voice on the loud speaker calling his name. Emily wandered away from the house when she was only three. It was the evening of our first night in a new house. Friends and family were everywhere, helping to unpack the kitchen, put towels in the bathroom, make beds and pillows available to us. When Emily's grandmother left to go pick up ten pizzas at the local pizzeria, no one noticed as Emily decided to follow her down the street, across the street, in the dark. It is an embarrassing story. When we gathered in the kitchen to say grace over the pizza, all wedged in and holding hands, I looked around the room, half counting heads and loving the friends and the house and the time together, and realized we were missing Emily. She was not in the kitchen. Not in the living room. Not in the bedrooms. Not in the attic. Not in the basement. What I remember of that night is only the sound of all my people calling her name. Some outside, some inside. And then a call to the police who told me Emily was sitting right there with them. An elderly couple that lived around the corner had found her, walking down the street. When they asked her where she lived, she couldn't answer. She was only three, and we had just moved in. She did tell them her "Grammy" had gone for pizza.

The truly strange thing about that night came when the police brought her to the house. They spoke to my embarrassment, saying, "Don't worry. It happens all the time." I thought they were lying to me, trying to comfort me. "Just keep an eye on her...she's a little wild child." I suspect that I remember these words with such clarity because they pointed me toward a fundamental truth: sooner or later all children will run off, disappear from view, and their parents will feel both fear and shame.

Searching for Our Children

So I imagine Mary and Joseph calling to Jesus. Standing perfectly still amidst an encampment of family and friends and calling out with their loudest voices. I imagine the sound as louder and clearer than any other moment in their lives with him, before or after. It is the steady shout of a child's name disappearing in the distance. When our kids are lost, we cry out from some place deep in the body, filled with breath, elongated with worry, and in the very cry of their names, we also wail a prayer. If no answer comes, we search.

Mary and Joseph searched as well. I imagine that they began with the help of friends and families, but before long, they were left alone to retrace their steps to Jerusalem, looking for him around corners, in shops, under stairwells. The support of their family and friends might have been useful. They could have set up a pattern for their search, separated, circled the city. But the story doesn't tell us that they all went looking, only Mary and Joseph. Despite all the expectations and all the presumptions about who he might be and where he might have gone, it still comes back to his parents. It is their job to find him. They must move through Jerusalem, looking at a once familiar city made strange by their searching. In contemporary families and faith communities, we assume, both jointly and individually, that schools, churches, neighbors, aunts, and uncles are paying attention to the needs of our youth. But in fact, everyone is making the same assumptions and it is through the cracks of that premise that youth slip away to find their own answers to their own questions.

Trusting the Village of Adults

I do believe the adage that it takes a village to raise a child. But, most of us don't live in villages, and even once we determine that a village would be a good place to live, we cannot find one, and don't know how to establish one. We live with locked doors—locked not only to strangers, but to our own next door neighbors. We are insulated in our homes and our cars and our routines, and we are hard pressed to let anyone into the day-to-day rhythms of our lives. My own experience in raising three children taught me the necessity of opening the door. I needed a village. And I got one.

At first, it was a difficult transition for me. I was raised in a family that not only locked the doors to strangers, but in some sense, locked each other out as well. I mean no disrespect to my family of origin because I am truly grateful for the gifts it gave to me. However, having an open door was not part of my childhood. For reasons too many to name, and maybe as simple as living in Detroit in the early 1960s and then moving because of job offers and opportunities throughout my childhood, we locked every door. My family, like every family, is the culmination and living expression of seen and unforeseen consequences. I grew up in a family that would never have doled out keys to friends. The gospel made me think it would be a good idea, and grace gave me the strength to give it a try.

The result was that my children grew up with people—in and out, around on the weekends, in for coffee, out for dinner, here, there, and everywhere. I counted on each of these people with keys to make a difference in the very quality of my time with my children. One taught us rudimentary American Sign Language. Another cooked dinner from the leftovers. Another helped with household chores. There was something magical about all the coming and going. Nevertheless, despite how present all of these folks were to me and to my children, there were still opportunities for my children to disappear into the culture at large. And my children have done their fair share of searching.

Jennifer met a group of friends at school who liked to hang out at a gas station in Hillsborough—about twenty miles from home. Emily loved to stay up late—her circadian rhythms make her the true night owl of the family—talking into the wee hours with friends, seeking answers on the Internet. Will had his own circle, too. He disappeared after his Junior Prom. I called ten parents, many of whom I had never met, before I found him. He was sleeping on the couch of a family I hardly knew. Every teen stretches the boundary in their own particular way. And in every case, with each of my children, I have had to go looking for them. The village established in and around my house was a great source of strength for me, but when push came to shove, they were not the ones who grounded my kids, restricted their movies, and set the limits. They were not called upon to search for the lost child. That job falls to parents alone. It was my challenge to figure out where to look, and sometimes that place is not a physical location.

Understanding Where Our Teenagers Find Understanding

Teenagers search the Internet, a virtual landmine of information out of context. They listen to music by bands I've never heard of. They go to the movies and watch HBO and Cinemax in the middle of the night.

They seek answers in whispered conversations with their friends. My own children were regularly exposed to a world of ideas and information, experiences and challenges that I could no longer easily find, control, or understand. For a period of about five years, when the children were younger, we went to the movies almost every Friday afternoon. But when they entered high school, suddenly they were going to the movies with their friends. We had always listened to music, from Kenny Loggins to Kenny Rogers, from show tunes to Sondheim, but when they reached high school, the music changed. They were listening with headphones to musicians and songwriters I had never heard of. This music didn't get much air time on the soft rock stations I listened to—or at least it seemed that way to me. When Will was nine, I took him with me on a long drive to Detroit. We sang along with tapes of familiar songs—and truly one of my dearest memories of him came on the last leg home, when he reached over, held my hand and sang, *"Now, I've had the time of my life…."* But when Will got to high school, all of a sudden he was listening to Incubus and Creed. *The Matrix* and *Cruel Intentions* were among his favorite movies. What happened?

No one in my village seemed to know the music or the movies any better than I did. They were ignorant of the lyrics to songs by Smashing Pumpkins or Ani DiFranco. We were all deaf and blind to the popular culture with which our own children were singing along, tapping their feet, and beginning to dance. It was Jennifer who introduced me to the Indigo Girls. Emily to Enya and Laurie Anderson. It was Will who made me listen to a CD of Creed.

I would never have gone there, into this new world of lyrics and ideas, if I hadn't been looking for my children. I wanted to see them in the light of what they were seeing. I wanted to hear what they were saying to themselves when no one was around. The way that I did it is certainly not the only way, but it was a good way. I asked them to show me. I changed the radio station on my car radio, and I started listening to what they were listening to. I make no claim to having seen all the movies that they've seen, nor have I listened to every song in their collections of CDs, but I did make a stab at it. And I am glad that I did.

When Mary and Joseph realized that they had lost their son somewhere along the way, they looked for him. When I realized that my own children were busily absorbing a world full of information, lyrics, images, and messages, I searched for them, too. I made it my business to get to know what Curt Kobain looked like, and what his music sounded like. I listened to Alanis Morrisette's *Jagged Little Pill*. Crash Test Dummies and *Mmmmm* changed my life. I memorized the lyrics to songs that I barely understood and intended to comprehend. I wanted to make sure that at least I knew the sound.

Along the way, I learned a lot. Not only about my children, but about the teen culture in general. Yes, some of it looks like a bad episode of talk TV. And yes, some of it is filled with the most violent and sexual content I could have imagined, and then some, but not all of it. I made it my business to consider how these poets and visionaries, the creators of teen culture, were coming into my home, and why my children were opening the door to them. Much of the why has been answered in the previous chapters—they were looking for the truth. The lyrics of a rock song have tremendous authority in the well-crafted mix of sixteen tracks, and the slick images of a multimillion dollar movie production look more real than reality. No wonder teens turn to it. Not only that, but the whole world of CDs, DVDs, and movies is marketed to teens. Why? Because most teens in America today have money in their pockets. My children were raised in the household of a working artist. Money was always tight, but nevertheless they each had birthday money, lunch money squirreled away in a bottom drawer, ten dollars here, twenty dollars there, and before I knew it, hundreds of CDs, half of which very few parents have ever heard. Now MasterCard and Visa are advertising debit cards for teens, so that no cash rests in their hands at all. I believe it is a marketing strategy designed to move young people into the world of instant gratification by means of credit and debt. *"Visa—its everywhere you want to be."* And teens want to be everywhere. How convenient. I am not saying that no one should give teens pocket money, but I do think that we should take a good long look at where they spend it and why they spend it where they do, and it wouldn't hurt if they were asked to earn more of it. It may help reduce some of the tension in the house if, when our children's ears are shrouded with headphones and a little of the baseline makes it out to us, we actually know the song they are listening to. It may be less terrifying to us if all of their recreational listening and viewing finds its balance in hard work for minimum wage.

Even in families where money is extremely tight, teens collect pirated copies of songs, make tapes from the radio, movies at other people's homes, and almost without spending a dime, view in full the world according to pop culture. They find pop culture and rap music and the Goths—those kids all dressed in black— and the drug culture and the steady voice of longing amplified in every direction.

When I was asked to speak at a national conference for Christian educators a few years ago, I was not surprised that very few recognized any of the songs I named while presenting my list of the top ten albums (showing my age in that descriptor) for spiritual reflection. Anything by Queen Latifa. Alanis Morrisette: *Jagged Little Pill* and *Supposed Former Infatuation Junkie*. Anything by REM and Michael Stipe. *Goodbye Jumbo* by World Party. Anything by Van Morrison: my favorite was *No Guru, No Method, No Teacher*. There were others. What did amaze me was the number of parents and people who work with teens week after week in youth groups and schools, who had never heard any of Queen Latifa's music. They knew her as a daytime talk show host. Many had never listened to a song called "With Arms Wide Open," about a young man who finds out he is the father of his girlfriend's child and prays that he will be able to raise his son to be a better man than he himself is. I understand that we might all rather listen to National Public Radio or the golden oldies station, but how will we learn if we never change the radio station? How will we hear what they hear if we lump all of the music our teens listen to into one category: bad? If we don't show some willingness to at least try to understand, how will they know it is safe to show us what moves them?

I am always surprised when Will brings me some new song to hear and it moves me. He sat by the radio one night when he was in the tenth grade to wait for a song that he wanted me to hear. The lyrics said:

> If I stay lucky then my tongue will stay tied
> and I won't admit the things that I hide.
> There are not enough years underneath this belt
> to make me admit the things that I felt.

Will is not a geek. He is not a nerd, nor is he a ne'er-do-well without friends. He just wanted to find a way to tell his mom that it is hard to be young, to know what to do, to say the right thing. He had to use a piece of the culture to tell me.

And I could tell comparable stories about Emily—and the rage she felt and let herself feel along with Alanis Morrisette when her first love went bad. I could talk about Jennifer and the way she used old Barbra Streisand songs to express her longing before puberty and how that longing evolved into her own dreams of fame and fortune in the music business. Jennifer works every weekend in her own band. She can sing covers from 1960 to 2000. During the week she teaches middle school and I imagine listens carefully to the references to singers and songwriters over school pizza in the cafeteria. Jennifer turned her adolescent angst into an endless critique—not only of content, but style as well.

Daring to Explore Our Teenagers' World

Faith gives us the courage to look inside, see, and recognize that there is something in the youth culture, something we ought to pay attention to. There are elements of truth in the music and the movies, even in the syntax, the rhymes, and the visual and musical treatments of a complexity that we need to hear, and feel, and memorize. These are the places our children are exploring and so we ought to explore them, too. I moved from the melodies and lyrics of Rodgers and Hammerstein to James Taylor, Bob Dylan, and Joni Mitchell, with a little Led Zeppelin thrown into the mix. My own children made a similar move. They left behind Gordon Lightfoot, Kenny Rogers, and James Taylor for Michael Jackson, Puff Daddy, and the Butchies.

If nothing else, it seems to me that every parent in America ought to go to the CD store at least once a year and listen to a cut from a few CDs on the display racks. Ask the clerk what's selling, and see what the bands are saying. Listen closely, and see what it is that young and not so young teens are buying. And before falling prey to a big reaction, listen closely to the longing, the heartache, the despair, the anger, and the desperate search for meaning, control, and power that fuels not only the lyrics, but the melody and the tempo. It will be worth it to listen to the pain and the anger. It will be worth it to find out what a band called Rage Against the Machine is raging against. If we listen long enough and with open hearts, we might begin to recognize that our own children are buying this music precisely because it expresses for them what they cannot yet express for themselves. It is hard to be alive right now. The old adages tell us: *the world is going to hell in a hand basket; no one said it would be easy; life sucks and then you die.* The adages survive because they are true, or at least true enough. The songs may also be providing our young people with ideas they have never before considered, both good and bad. The ideas may be familiar to us but foreign to them. It is just as possible that these ideas about love and life, lust and self-gratification may have already become familiar to them, while they remain foreign to us. In either case, we cannot speak to what we do not know.

I learned something in all of this listening. I learned that my own children, no matter how deeply I had loved them, how thoroughly I cared for them, how completely I provided for them, still had to face the world on their own. They had to find their own voices. They had to find sufficient strength to be themselves and immediate comfort when faced with disappointment. I continue to learn every time I allow myself to listen to what teenagers listen to. I learn some things about them, and I learn about myself. If nothing else, I learn more about the culture at large as viewed through the eyes of one barely old enough to imagine unforeseen consequences, much less live with them.

Several years ago, I taught at a charter school whose population was made up of kids who can only be described as troubled or gifted or both. They were drop outs, many without parents. Several of the students were homeless and slept in cars. One day, as I came out of my classroom, several kids were waiting in the hall. One grabbed the headset off another, handed it to me, and said, "Miss Amanda, you've got to listen to this." I listened. It was filled with the harshest sexual and violent content I had ever heard. The young woman looked at me. I got down close to her, looked her in the eye and whispered, "Why are you listening to this?" She didn't answer. "What are you getting from listening to this?" The boy who handed it to me said, "That's what I'm saying." She just looked at me. I said, "Once you get those ideas in there, it's hard to get them out." Still, she did not respond.

Several months later, she stopped me in the same hallway and asked if we might talk for a minute. She took a deep breath and blurted out a story. Two years earlier, when she was fourteen, she had been gang raped by a group of her friends. She wanted me to know. Why had she been listening to that music? I can't be certain, but I suspect that something about its raging violence made her feel less alone in the secret she was carrying. In listening to just a few of the lyrics in that one song, I moved a step closer to knowing the heart of that young woman's longing. She wanted to be known. She wanted to be forgiven.

Loving Our Teenagers Enough to Dare to Ask the Questions

Even if the problem is not so severe, even if its just soft pornography tucked between the mattress and the bed frame or lyrics hallmarked by depression, someone needs to be asking our children why they are looking at it and listening to it. It is not enough to ban these things from our homes. Someone needs to speak directly to our kids, with full knowledge of the content and more experience in living with it. We need to tell our young people that objectifying human beings for momentary pleasure is a sin and an expensive one. We need to say with as much patience and compassion as we can muster, "Why are you listening to that? What are you getting from it?" Someone needs to speak directly to the questions and the longing and the desire and the pain.

I believe that someone needs to be us. It may be that young people will confess their longings first through the words of the music they listen to, and it may be that they will tell a teacher or a youth group leader long before they tell their parents, but still, they need to speak what is true, some one needs to listen and answer...one way or the other.

And I suppose that the same thing can be said for movies. Why would *The Matrix* be among Will's favorite movies? Maybe it's because the movie articulates (however erroneously) how impossibly dreamlike this world seems. Maybe because we have come dangerously close to living in a culture that possesses no clear hierarchy of meaning—no sense of what really matters. I know that building that hierarchy is a part of what must be accomplished in teen development. I know that it is normal, all a part of the plan. But it seems undeniable to me that the plan also requires that someone, and more specifically, some faith-filled adult, find the courage, not only to go looking for our children in the midst of this dangerous culture, but also to speak directly to the pitfalls they face, the lies they hear, the loneliness they feel, and the pains they hide. Someone needs to find them and speak to them with both the love and the authority that only time and relationships can generate. It is not enough to let our children be guided through adolescence by the strangers who live in our culture. We must add our voices to the mix.

As I write this I realize that there are millions of young people who are good kids, who have never looked at pornography or listened to violent lyrics. They have never smoked pot or tried ecstasy or had sex or done anything wrong at all. At least that's what so many people tell me. Defensively they say, "not all kids are bad." But I am not suggesting that kids are bad at all. My own children are not bad. The girl who told me about the gang banging, and even the gang-bangers themselves are not inherently bad. They are sinful, yes, but not bad, and there is a difference.

Infinitely Worthy of Our Attention

I am suggesting that our teenagers are infinitely good and worthy of our attention. We, the adults in this complex and shifting system we call modernity, have failed to do our part if we refuse to attend to the world in which our young people are living. We have failed if we do not get to know it: the hidden hallways, the dark corners, the stairs that lead to places we have never even imagined. The kids we love so much or so little, those we like so deeply and worry so much about, and even those who have hurt us or others with such force that we can barely speak to them, much less guide them, they are living together with us in the very same culture. We are all exposed to things which require the passionate faith-filled engagement of others in order to be better understood.

It would be easy but nevertheless fruitless to merely curse the culture. It is wiser to engage it, speak to it, and ultimately baptize it in the waters of God's loving intervention. I may have ten albums that are my top picks for spiritual reflection, but what really matters is not which albums I choose, nor which movies or magazines. What matters is that I be willing to take a chance and to see what my teenagers choose: to read the magazines, to watch the movies, to hear the rhythms, to pay attention to the words and in the discipline of doing so, to discover a way that the good news of God might speak with knowledge and authority into the messages our culture preaches.

It is not easy to be this type of parent. I knew at the time, and I know now, that policing with a strong set of laws and restrictions regarding what my children could and could not see or hear could be minimally effective, at best. For every new rule I established, I knew they had ample opportunity to go outside my arm's reach in order to meet their objectives. It seems that the only chance we have to make sense of the craziness that our children experience is to be careful to experience it with them, not with unyielding judgment, but with compassion. Judgment must be tempered with mercy. Rules must be balanced with relationships.

I think of Jesus, later in his life, sitting with the sinners and the tax collectors, eating meals with the harlots and the evil doers. I cannot believe that the whole of their discourse centered on things spiritual. Jesus was a great storyteller and he was a great listener. He is the model for parents as well. Yes, we need to inform, but we also need to be informed. Yes, we need to correct, but we also need to listen carefully in order that we might correct at the deepest level.

Imagining All That We Might Never See

At first glance, all of this may seem far removed from the story in the gospel. Too easily do we tell ourselves that the world in which Jesus lived was far safer than our own. The gospel stories provide no hint that Jesus did anything but tarry in Jerusalem. But in itself, this notion of tarrying makes me wonder what he did as he tarried. Did he go directly to the Temple? What did he see and experience along the way? There is no way to know the answer. But this I know for sure, Jesus was a teenager—a young boy with questions and answers in his heart. I am certain that however he made his way to the Temple, he did so with his eyes wide open and his attention piqued by all that happened around him. I feel confident that as Mary and Joseph explored the city in their search, they were just as offended by what they saw and heard as I have been by so much of what I saw and heard in my own search for my children. The truly frightening part is that no matter how much we see, there is still more that we might never see.

In much the same way that we cannot know precisely where Jesus was, or how he came to the Temple, likewise, no matter how diligently we attempt to see and understand the dangerous culture in which our children move, we will still be left to imagine. We can inform our imaginations with contemporary lyrics and movies, as I have suggested, but we will also have to imagine our own particular sons' and daughters' reactions on any particular day.

Imagination relies on knowledge creatively reconstructed into a simple or an elaborate picture that expands beyond the simple facts. The more knowledge we have, the more elaborate the picture. As we imagine Jesus at age twelve, we inform those images with all that we know about the life and ministry of the Christ. We temper our vision of him at twelve, with knowledge of his life as a whole. We add details from snippets of stories we remember about him. Perhaps he saw the sick and the castaways that would later become the recipients of his miracles. Perhaps he watched a woman search the ground around her feet for a lost coin, dropped in the midst of a purchase. Perhaps he saw the untouchables of his day, begging at the gate. We use what we know of Jesus to imagine what these particular days might have been like. We add to that our knowledge of Middle Eastern culture and cuisine. We smell the spices and the roasted meats. We recall the taste of humus and flat breads.

When we attempt to imagine where our own children are, or what they may be thinking and feeling as they move through their own culture, we do not have the luxury of knowing the whole story. Our imaginations are easily informed by fear and doubt. We run every fear-filled scenario with picture perfect focus. We doubt that our young people even know that a temple still exists, much less, how to get there. Yet, even in this imagining, we can take comfort because Mary and Joseph were left to imagine, too. They did not have the benefit of a completed canon of Scriptures about their son, anymore than we can read ahead in the life stories of our children. Yes, Mary and Joseph had hopes and expectations about who he was and who he ought to become. Yes, they may have remembered something of the promises and miracles that surrounded his coming into the world, but the details of his sacrifice were unknown to them in much the same way that the particularities of our own children's impending sacrifices and offerings to the world are unknown to us.

The Only Solution

They knew only this: he was lost to them. Nothing could be worse. And they knew that there could be no solution but to look for him.

We are in the same position as our children reach adolescence. There is no solution but to look for them. They may or may not be literally lost to us. They may be no farther away than their own bedrooms, with the doors closed, but make no mistake, they are on the path to their own destiny. Our task is to be brave enough to look without allowing fear to generate only the worst case scenario. If we are not careful, our fears will only serve to silence our children when they are in our presence. We must also be brave enough to ask questions and listen carefully to the answers. Without accusing them, we must ask, "Why are you listening to that? What do you like about that movie?" And when they begin to answer, we will have to set aside our passels of definitive answers as well as our own ignorance if we are to hear their replies. We barely listen to the answers our teens offer. We write their insights off when compared to our own. We have to learn as well as remember. Listen carefully as well as lecture.

Imagination is more than knowledge stirred with creativity; it is also an expression of our memories. We stir into our fears for our children every memory we have of our own adolescent journey. We may have been the best kids or the worst, or some mix of both, but each of us carries into adulthood a series of memories shaped in the teen years. The person that I was in my teen years is still alive and kicking in my adult life. I only have to remember her in order to recognize all the ways that those memories continue to shape my life. I need to remember my own loves and longings, my own rebellion and my own challenges of truth in order to honor the love, longing, rebellion, and challenge my own children face. When we imagine where our children are—what they are doing, seeing, listening to—we must be diligent, as Mary and Joseph were diligent. We must look for as long as it takes to find not only the young person we seek, but a deeper understanding of the territory through which they have traveled.

Finally, lest someone accuse me of wanting to be "buddy-buddy" with my kids, or wanting to be "cool" and "with it" in order to become every teenager's favorite mom, it seems important to add one more thing to this exploration of the culture and the community. My children, like all children, needed a parent, not another friend. They needed someone who was able to set curfews and listen long enough to their music, watch enough of their movies, and travel the same roads not so that they could stay safe within the confines of my home and the insights of my reflections but rather, so that they could know that there was nothing happening in their lives that could significantly alter my affection for them or destroy my dedication to their well-being.

I have often thought that parents (and teachers and youth leaders) must be like the Holy Spirit in their vigilance. We will not leave our young people comfortless. Our youth may leave us for a time and refuse the comfort that we offer. The result may well be a frantic day or two, a horrible year, but we must not be the ones who left. We must be the ones who are ever present, reminders of the loving presence of God.

I am suggesting that we must be the ones who offer to our young people a compassionate ear as they listen to music we truly despise—because, in the listening, we might once or twice be given the opportunity to explain why we hate that music and discover why they do not. We must be the presence that understands and critiques the slimy, slick images that come out of Hollywood—because, by our presence, we might, just once or twice, be given the opportunity to discuss the things that the entertainment media offer and remind our young people that reality is better than movies, always, no matter what.

We may not find our lost ones right away, but like the hound of heaven, like the Holy Spirit herself, we will be steadily moving towards them, even as they tarry behind in Jerusalem. It's a tall and tender order. We will not leave our young people lost, but rather, like Mary and Joseph before us, we will search for them. It is a solemn vow, taken with little or no assurance that we will receive the desired outcome. We do not know the full destiny of our children. But, like Mary and Joseph before us, come hell or high water, committed to the faith formation of our teens, we will not leave them comfortless. Isn't this the way of compassion?

Twenty years after being lost in Jerusalem, Jesus spoke to his followers about the lost sheep and the good shepherd. I wonder if he remembered his mom and dad then, and the look on their faces when they saw him in the Temple after three days of searching for him. I wonder if he remembered what he might have learned that day. Love always looks for the lost and continues to look until love finds its beloved. This is compassion then: to set aside our disappointment in the well-meaning community and to look past our fear of the culture. We are not looking to critique or condemn. We are looking for a child of God. Like Mary, like Joseph, and like the Good Shepherd himself, we must look for the lost and continue to look until love finds its beloved.

chapter four

The Time It Takes to Find

Only in community
does the person appear
in the first place,
and only in community
can the person
continue to become.

Parker Palmer

VEN THOUGH THE WRITINGS of theologians are rarely
intended for mass consumption, the primary goal
of virtually all theological writing is to offer a way
of approaching, defining, and then putting our faith
into action. We do this in order to find grace, meaning,
and comfort in our lived-experience. Theology helps us
to structure our lives in community by creating a set of
expectations through which every member can find
and follow a common set of disciplines. Despite what I
consider an unquestionable need for this sort of

definition, for most of us the idea of a theology of adolescence seems remote and perhaps unnecessary. Very few would say that we structure our interactions with teenagers by means of our theology.

Over the past decade, it has become increasingly clear to me that when we find ourselves the parents of teenagers, there is little to offer much hope, or structure, or assurance. The language of lived faith and the idiom of the theologians rarely jibe, and the rules of monastic orders were never designed to accommodate the needs of a family system. Parents and educators are left to wait and hope for a sermon or two in the course of the church year that might focus on the needs of teens. We anticipate the chance to listen to an expert, and more often than I care to imagine, we end up relying on TV talk shows or radio call-in shows for the best glimpse into the mysterious world of adolescence. As a culture, we have neither a working understanding of what it means to be a teenager today, nor a vocabulary of faith to inform the process. We end up fixated on fixes—the quicker the better.

The Ill-defined Terrain of Adolescence

The problem is this: the transition from childhood to adulthood takes both time and intention. We do not become adults merely by making it through the teen years. We do not become adults when our bodies are tall enough, our hormones are flowing, or we finish college. We become adults in the world when our communities recognize that we have become a force to be reckoned with in all the best possible meanings of the phrase. We become adults when we make it through the Red Sea, cross the mighty wilderness, and enter into the land that was promised to us as children—a promised land full not only of milk and honey, but giants and struggles and conflicts which we are, in fact and in truth, prepared to face. We don't get there automatically, and we do not get there alone.

In the United States today, adolescence is an unwieldy and ill-defined period of life. It is also remarkably lonely. In part, this is due to the fact that we lack a clear understanding of the developmental and spiritual concerns of our teens. We are unsure when adolescence begins and even less sure of when it might end. We share little, if any, sense of what tasks must be accomplished and what goals realized in the meantime. We tentatively agree that the transition has something to do with the size and shape of our bodies and perhaps with a willingness to take at least minimal responsibility for our actions. We even say that the goal of adolescence is to "find yourself." As soon as that is done, whatever all that means, we nod a little and say, "Okay, perhaps our children are no longer children." The whole process lasts for an indeterminate amount of time—somewhere between seven and seventeen years, give or take a couple of decades. In a very real sense, for many people, it never ends.

From a developmental standpoint, adolescence begins with the onset of puberty, itself a shifting target. At the time of this writing, for females, the average age for the on-set of menses is eleven years, nine months and getting younger all the time. Males also enter this puberty zone before they turn thirteen. As a culture, and as a faith, we are remarkably silent about the changes our bodies undergo and the myriad implications of these changes on our relationships and our future. From beginning to end, the process takes many years, and happens at a slightly different pace in each individual. For so many young people the whole process of puberty—the changes in hormone levels and all that they bring with them, changes in the body and changes in the heart—happens in a shroud of secrecy. Very few adults are willing to talk about the "facts of life," let alone how rich a time of life young people are entering. It seems that no one mentions that the changes must take place with adult companionship.

I remember when Will, my youngest, took the short course on human development offered in the fifth grade.

We discussed his participation, and I signed the consent form, with his consent in place as well. I imagined it couldn't hurt, and if we were lucky it might afford us some opportunities to talk about what he was learning and how it might be understood in the context of a life of faith. When he came home after the first day and said, "It was gross! If all of that is going to happen to me, I don't want any of it," I thought, "And who can blame him?" When you learn the technical aspects of the anticipated changes in your physical body, and you learn them in the context of a scientific model in a public school classroom, why would anyone think that it was going to be fun? Interesting? Exciting? Cool? Much less, Holy?

You wouldn't. You can't. For these insights we need theology.

As Will spoke, I imagined him, seated in the darkened classroom, watching an array of full color slides, simple cartoons of human bodies, charts of female and male reproductive systems, and no one to talk to about the depth of change, the slow-motion pace at which it occurs, and the incredible power and blessing that these changes will bring with them. It seems as if no one wants to mention to kids how rich a time of life this is, how thoroughly the heartaches are worth the new power. No one tells them that all of this is good. Absolutely, entirely, wonderfully good. At least no one tells them in ways that they can understand. We may chime in about teen years being the best years of your life (which is something of a lie), but we forget to talk about the costly process of moving from childhood to adolescence, the losses and fears, and the stretch and pull of muscles as they grow, sinews as they lengthen, hearts and minds as they expand.

Imagining a Theology of Adolescence

We fail to do so because we lack a theology for this transition. We have a theology for death, so we are able to comfort the grieving. We have a theology for marriage, so we are able to counsel the engaged. We lack a theology of adolescence and are tongue-tied because of it. Good theology will give us a way to have candid and merciful conversation regarding the vast array of changes that constitute this particular time in the human life cycle. Yes, we do want to talk, at least a little, about hair under your arms, pubic hair, hair on your legs, and back, and, yes, that whole menstruation and production of live sperm thing. We want to talk about it, because in relationships where compassion is the guiding principle, we won't let difficulty or shame keep us from facing up to the mysterious.

Good theology makes it possible to interpret changes in the body as a window onto changes in the heart. We may want to believe that the body and the spirit of a human being are somehow two distinct entities, but our theology of Incarnation, in which we confess belief in the person of Jesus, fully human and fully divine, presses us to remember that as surely as Jesus was fully human and fully divine, so, too, are we one lovely and frightening mishmash of heart and mind, body and spirit. We are enmeshed, intermingled, unified, one. When something is happening in the body, it is also happening in the spirit. When something happens in the mind, it also happens in the heart.

All of this matters when considering ways to manage, survive, and even deepen our compassion for young people and their journeys through adolescence. The more firmly we can establish a theology, a basic understanding of the process of maturation, and set aside the notion that it will all happen as a matter course, the more readily we will be able to face and speak to the deeper concerns of the heart. There is no single, definitive, and uniformly applicable process, but we can watch the transformation with the eyes of faith, and we can engage the concerns our children face with the authority of love.

Over the course of a few short years, my children were literally transformed by the changes wrought in adolescence. They looked one way when they were nine and ten, and completely another by the time they were sixteen and seventeen. If I hadn't been there to slowly and steadily observe the changes, I might not have recognized them.

But even more significant than the physical changes were the emotional and spiritual changes that took place. It was not enough to merely watch this change. My theology demanded that I participate in it: marvel at how tall they were getting, pay attention when deodorant was tossed into the grocery cart with an underhand pitch to rival the all-stars, and ask them if they need anything from the drug store (and be sure to get it when they ask). Razors, tampons, shampoos, aftershave, all of the basic hygiene products that suddenly seem to flood the house are reminders of what is happening to our children. But buying the accouterments is not the same thing as engaging the questions. It was far more challenging to engage their questions of faith. There was nothing to purchase on a drug store shelf that would aid me in this. I had to look within, pray a lot, and listen carefully before speaking.

I am not entirely sure what makes conversations about these things seem so unwieldy, but I am nevertheless convinced that they need to happen—in the car, at the kitchen counter, in the living room, in the hall. These conversations are not necessarily going to be full-blown in-depth inquiries into the details of faith, much less the details of physical changes, but rather, the parent will maintain a consistently kind presence. A good theology for adolescence must begin with the assertion that faith formation and personal maturation cannot happen in a vacuum. Parents have a primary role to play even in the smallest things.

Adult Involvement in Adolescence

It is my belief that by including ourselves in the work of this transformation, we can fulfill our obligation to bring the good news of God to bear on our young people's lives. Among the central tenets of our faith is the truth of God's love: God so loved the world that he gave his one and only Son (John 3:16). We model something essential to Christian theology when we give ourselves to the lives of our young people. Absolutely. God cares about every detail of your life. Certainly God doesn't care about which brand of toothpaste you use, but the Christian tradition is one in which the principles of intimate involvement and close camaraderie are essential if we are to fulfill the call of the gospels. If parents miss the opportunity to model this involvement and camaraderie in the details of an everyday life, then young people may well be left with the illusion that there are arenas within their lives where they are entirely alone and without advocate or assistance. We are there to aid, to pray, to talk, to cheer our young people on as they make this change in life. At every step, we are helping our young people to become more and more competent, more and more capable of managing the demands of adulthood.

Still, with all the physical changes and the new potentials, no one becomes an adult until understanding and managing the changes in the body inform the concomitant changes in the heart and spirit. I have a theory that much of young people's infamous "acting out" has little to do with an intent to anger parents or even to express adolescent angst but has everything to do with trying to find the line, the point at which they will finally be held responsible for the quality of their own lives. In the process, they are left far too alone and without the necessary reminders of their parents' love and dedication. Because we live in a culture which does not have a clear boundary between childhood and adulthood, and because we are lacking a clear theology of adolescence through which we might define and delineate the edges of each phase in life, our teenagers are left to determine independently exactly what it takes to cross over. Parents must intervene, participate, accompany, witness, and acknowledge the change from child to adult.

But when, exactly, will this happen? For most of us, the answer is, "Who knows?" Little if any conversation happens in families, or churches, schools, or youth groups about the richness of this transformation. We do not have a handy framework within which to hold this kind of conversation. For most of the late twentieth century, the church has relied on confirmation in some form as a puberty rite. As such, it cannot help us frame a discussion of adulthood, because it is a sacrament afforded to early and preteens. After confirmation, there is no ongoing dialogue about young adult faith. And yet, in the middle teen years, from fourteen to nineteen, faith formation is at its most tender. The church has been consistently silent on these issues, and the community at large is conflicted. There is no ready pattern, and we are reluctant to establish one for a variety of reasons ranging from ignorance to indifference to exhaustion. We may ask, "What is happening?" and "How long will it take?" But there are few clear answers to our questions.

Looking to the culture at large, the legal age of majority is eighteen for some things and twenty-one for others. Eighteen-year-olds can vote, and it is legal to drink at twenty-one. A sixteen-year-old can earn a driver's license, but in many states that privilege is now linked to attendance and grade point averages in high school. If the student fails or drops out, they lose the privilege of mobility, and often lose the possibility of finding a job, earning their keep, and contributing to the community along with it. In some states, with parental permission, a fourteen-year-old can marry. But, I have never met a parent who was whole-hearted in their belief that a married fourteen-year-old has instantaneously become an adult. Even the creation of a child will not move the average teen across the invisible boundary of childhood into adulthood.

Whenever I meet a young person who seems too old for their years, I wonder, "Who 'parentified' you? Who left you on your own in ways that forced you to take on behaviors and responsibilities for which you were ill prepared?" Perhaps it would be better if I were to ask, "What community reared, raised, and readied this child for adulthood?" In my heart, I wonder what tears are shed in this young person's room for all the lost chances to try things out, to change, and to test the waters within the context of the family before it mattered so much? As a culture, we aren't sure what constitutes adulthood, and therefore we aren't sure when or how it happens or what role adults play in the process.

The Transition to Adulthood: When and How Does It Happen?

Over the past ten years, I have read and studied as deeply as I could in order to learn about the rituals that surround the transition from childhood to adulthood in various cultures around the world and throughout recorded history. What I found was a wealth of information about these rites of passage, but virtually none of them have been fully integrated into our contemporary, post-industrial society. Unlike our ancestors, and unlike our contemporaries in other cultures, we cannot pinpoint a day when parents and faith community join to acknowledge the transition from child to adult. We don't know when it happened to us, and we sure as heck don't know when it will happen for our own children.

Nevertheless, in my conversations with adult youth leaders and parents around the country, consistent themes have emerged. Many have said they became adults on their wedding day. But when asked when they feel a young person might be truly ready for marriage, most answer that they, themselves, were well into their twenties when they got married, and were, nevertheless, unprepared. As a culture, we are delaying marriage overall, until both partners are financially independent, live on their own, and have meaningful work. We assert that these are necessary precursors to entering a marriage with our eyes wide open, with some experience of life under our belts. We even say that it is just common sense. But historically, people married without so many precursors, and much younger. No matter how big the bank account and the credit line, we all know lots of married people who are still "kids at heart." And we don't mean it in the playful sense. We mean immature. Sometimes the marriage lasts; sometimes it doesn't. Either way, saying "I do" doesn't transform anyone into a grown up.

When I ask these groups to consider when they became adults, there is always one person who answers, "I'm still a kid!" or "I'm still trying to figure out what I'm going to do when I grow up." and everyone laughs (and it is usually a middle-aged man who announces this). We laugh because we recognize the feeling. The truth is, he is announcing something very real, very close to the bone for many adults in America. We are a culture which lacks the clarity of rituals to define a beginning, middle, and end to adolescence. We spend as much as half of our adult lives wondering if we've made it. Are we there yet? Is it over now? Am I a grown up? When midlife comes, we are shocked—choking at the passage of time, suddenly thrust into a midlife crisis which, in all likelihood, resembles our adolescent experience in significant measure.

How do we make the transition from child to adult?

In this post-industrial age, when we are living longer, and staying healthier than ever before, and have seemingly limitless options for constructing a life, it is a terribly complicated problem. Do we become adults when we leave home? Or when we have to pay our own way? Or when we have children of our own? Some say that the armed forces will make a grown-up out of you. Others say that it happens when you graduate from college. All of these answers seem insufficient. Someone might say, "Well, you become a grown up when all sorts of things conspire against you and force you to face up to the life you have made and are living." It is a sort of "You've made your bed. Now, lie in it." approach.

As near as I can tell, in America today, children become adults when they survive the rigors of an undefined journey from dependency to independence. To put it in simpler terms, they become themselves when they find themselves. What a sloppy self-initiation! Without rites of passage, without ritual, without adult mentors, without a theology of adolescence, we blunder along until...when? Until we find ourselves? Not only has no culture ever asked its youth to stay young for so long, but no previous generation of adults has been so firmly committed to the notion that children need to be lost in adolescence in order to "find themselves."

Raising Adults

In order to answer the confusion and give structure to the experience, we must go back to the gospels and look for hints and guideposts that will serve us in our experience. We must look and see if Jesus was lost and then found himself. What exactly happened in this story and what impact might the story have on how we parent? In the gospel, Jesus was lost for three days. Even if we allow for the possibility that the number was used as a kind of storytelling code indicating a complete unit of time, Jesus did not "find himself." His parents found him, and the elders protected him from the greatest danger of all: wandering aimlessly through this gift of a life, trying to piece together a sense of self without context, without guidance, and without meaning. In listening to the story, we find that Jesus was not part of a lost generation.

We rightly call our teenagers part of a lost generation, but only because we have relinquished the most fundamental responsibility of parenthood—the making of adults. It is not enough to raise children. We must raise adults. To leave our teens alone in the time in life when the human body undergoes the most profound changes, while their peers wander beside them (the blind leading the blind), while plagued by the imaginary audience, while creating the self, and while sprouting underarm hair, to leave them wandering aimlessly and without guidance and advocacy is a sin. It is a recipe for disaster.

For want of a theology, adolescence has become a roundabout romp and a lonely pilgrimage through the wilderness. There is no pillar of fire to guide them; there is no manna in this wilderness. There is no hope of crossing over. Our children leave the nest and begin the search. They get lost, and if lucky, find themselves along the way. What is most troubling is that parents participate in this madness, firmly believing and all but insisting that our children need to go off and find out who they are. So many parents say that teens need to leave the church in order to discover what they believe. Parents actively advocate for self-discovery as though that could possibly be accomplished in a vacuum. Just because parents are not there does not mean that young people are completely alone. There are so many other forces. Parents tell themselves that if teens succeed in this crazy effort, then they will return to us as adults, friends, strangers, and we will be so glad to see them again.

But this is not the way of the gospel. The gospel teaches that while Jesus was lost, his parents sought to find him. While Jesus was lost, the elders engaged him and he sat with them on the Temple steps. While Jesus was lost, he was not, in fact, alone. And nothing in the gospel implies that testosterone levels or the mere passage of time made the difference for Jesus. What did make the difference was the willingness of his parents to search for him for as long as it took to find him. What made a difference was the passionate engagement of other adult members of the community who, by their presence, aided him in his development. He did not have to find himself, he had to be found. The responsibility to move from childhood to adulthood was not his alone. That responsibility was shared between self, family, and faith community.

For many years I have tried to understand how this might be applied to my life as a parent, and in some sense this is the greatest mystery.

From Adolescence to Adulthood: What's Got to Happen?

I want to suggest that two significant things must occur in order for adolescence to end and adulthood to begin. First, the young person must be able to acknowledge the gift of their own life and take responsibility for it in all its complexity. This knowledge must be tried and tested, challenged and scrutinized until at some fundamental level, the individual can say with at least a modicum of assurance that they know who they are and what they believe. As in the life of Jesus, there will come a time when all the questions of who we are, what we want, and what we intend to do about it become vital and crucial. In the life of Jesus, this happens in the Temptation narrative. He is tempted to be someone other than who he really is. He is challenged to interpret the meaning of the stories of faith as they might apply to him personally. He answers the questions with not only the "right" answers, all of which are drawn from the stories of his faith heritage, but with a deep understanding that allows that right answer to be truly his, spoken in his own authentic voice. He would never have been able to accomplish the mysteries of his ministry if he had not internalized a sense of his own authority. This is the first step toward full adulthood. Our young people must find their own voices and speak the truth with authority. Neither can happen if they are left alone too soon. Preparation must be made for the challenges they will undoubtedly face.

Second, the family and community of origin must also recognize and embrace the newly discovered self of the young person and welcome that person into the complex task of making and building a whole new life within watch of the community. When the Scriptures tell us that Jesus grew in favor with God and man, it is the presence of both God and man that makes the growth meaningful. The significance of the miracle at the wedding of Cana in Galilee, the first miracle recorded in John's gospel, may lie in the context more than in the action of changing water to wine. Perhaps it is safe to assume that this is the true coming of age story in John, for here we see Jesus, in relationship to the Creator, the community, and his own mother, acting as his true self. I am suggesting that the transformation from child to adult requires the participation of the self, parents, the community, and God interacting together in one time and one place. The story closes with this sentence: "He thus revealed his glory, and his disciples put their faith in him" (John 2:11b). Is it too much for us, as parents, to seek opportunities when our children, like Jesus, will reveal their true nature, and in that moment earn the respect and regard of the community? I think not. This is what parents must learn to expect.

The question of when this transformation is complete remains open for reflection and debate. However, the Scriptures offer two clues. First, it does not happen in three days. Jesus does not enter the Temple as a boy and leave as a man. It would be folly to think so, and it would place an undo burden on our young people to anticipate any such overnight transition. In truth, the passageway from child to adult has no set boundaries. It does not necessarily begin at puberty or end at age twenty-one. The mystery lies in the very fact that this transition requires holy time far more than a stopwatch. It will not necessarily conform itself to any preconceived timeline.

Luke employed the "three day" rule—saying that Mary and Joseph searched for him for three days. We can infer an important truth from this: it takes a complete unit of time to learn these lessons and begin the process. Three, like seven and like forty, is one of the numbers used in our Scriptures to speak of complete units of time. And while even I will admit that three days is a long time to search for a lost child, it is a relatively short time when compared to the decades of searching so many young people endure in an effort to find themselves. When parents fall into despair over struggles with their teens, it is helpful to remember that the decade from ten to twenty years of age, the decade in which all of this change is occurring, is but a small part of the whole scope of our lives. Even more, the particular conflicts and patterns that we set in our adolescence are not, in fact, binding. For most people, adolescence is neither the best, nor the worst, time in life. We continue to learn as we age. We continue to change and grow. In fact, much of adolescence is not particularly significant at all. Many teens are quick to point out that they are bored. Who can blame them? Because we have extended the teen years, and because we aren't clear about the challenges, goals, and end results, we leave our teenagers hanging out, wondering what is expected of them, and when will it be their turn?

The second hint comes clear when we recognize that Jesus may have begun to understand who he was in the Temple, talking to the elders, but he still had to answer to his parents. We tend to put the process of becoming an adult somewhere outside the influence of family and faith community. Yet in the life of Jesus, the transition from "child of Mary and Joseph" to "Savior and Redeemer of the world" is not completed until much later in the gospels when Jesus stands firm in the face of evil, when the elders recognize him as a threat, when his mother acknowledges his capacity to change water into wine, when his friends realize that they cannot stand with him through the long hours of his prayers.

The Context of Transformation

We become adults within a context, and as in all contexts, it takes time to make meaningful changes.

Young people need to assert their understanding and their right to greater freedom and intentionality. At the same time parents and trusted members of the community need to lovingly call these same rights and assertions back into a living context, questioning both their meanings and their consequences. Mary wasn't thrilled when she found Jesus in the Temple. Some might even say she was angry with him. "How could you? Didn't you know your father and I were worried about you? Anxiously searching for you?" In the Temple, Jesus answers in what almost sounds like a surprised and defensive posture, "Didn't you know? How could I be anywhere else?"

That is part of the necessary transition. If American culture tends to define adulthood in terms of personal autonomy and independence, then faith-filled parents must stand up and say, "No!" Adulthood is earned when youth and parents alike establish ways to be inter-dependent. It is earned when we learn how to be responsible for and accountable to one another. This is the most mysterious part of the gospel story. Mary asserts her responsibility and insists on Jesus' accounta-bility, and he agrees to it—but not without asserting his own responsibilities and insisting on Mary's accounta-bility to that as well. Adulthood is not defined by full and complete independence from parents and elders and other members of the community. Faithful adulthood rests in relationships, in this willingness to be inter-dependent, to care for the self *and* others, to be trust-worthy in our dealings, not only with what we want and need, but with the implications and concerns that our needs raise in the context of family and community.

Perhaps then we can define true adulthood as this delicate balance between personal authority and inter-dependence. We become adults when we are able to balance the needs and dreams of the self with the reality of the community. We become adults when our individ-uated concerns extend from the narcissism of our individuality to include a deep regard for the life of the whole family, community, and the world in which we live.

None of this can happen, the process cannot be completed until parents and other faithful adults stand there, take on all the pain, all the discomfort, all the concern, and watch for the adult to emerge from the child. The community must insist on finding this young person who is so busily engaged in trying to find herself, and we must refuse to believe that "finding yourself" is a good way to spend your life.

All of this might seem rather amorphous, but that is entirely my point. There is a unique transition that each young person must make if they are to move from childhood to adulthood. How long might this transition last? The only realistic answer is, "as long as it takes." The gospel story does not tell us that one day Jesus was a child and three days later he was an adult. There is no magic number, no prescribed amount of time.

The Parent's Role in the Transition to Adulthood

Rather than asking how long will this take, we might ask, "What is my role as a parent in this transition? What can I do to help my young person make this move?" I am suggesting three key things.

First, *parents must raise adults.*

Despite the way our culture looks at this, it is parents who must create the tension necessary for growth. The Scripture says that Jesus grew in favor with God and man after he came under the authority of his mother and father and was obedient to them. His parents raised him by raising the responsibilities and expectations. As freedom and hormone levels increased, so did his capacity to contribute to the life of the family. I understand that it is not considered "normal" to ask what contributions to the life of the family teenagers will be expected to make. Most of the parents I have spoken with say that their teen's only "job" is to do well in school. Is that sufficient? In every other culture in the history of the world, seventeen-year-old boys would have been giving significant amounts of their labor and resources to their family. Our teenage boys are not afforded that luxury. And I do mean luxury. There is a comfort, consolation, and grace that can only be experienced when you come to understand that you have a vital role to play in the survival and sustenance of the people with whom you live. These responsibilities and expectations may be in constant flux, but nevertheless they should be clearly stated, talked about and agreed upon. There should be more chores that support the life of the family, more time together engaged in meaningful work, and greater consequences when teens fail to contribute in agreed upon ways.

When my Jennifer was a teenager, we spent a day listing all the expectations I had for her on a 5x7 note card. On the back we wrote all the expected consequences if she failed to meet the expectations. While I don't think we ever actually used the lists, working on it together, working it out together, helped both of us to navigate the stormy waters of her adolescence. We talked about what was fair and unfair and why. We talked about chores and curfews before they were set and why we were setting them at that level. The conversations were uncomfortable and difficult, but in doing it, we set a pattern for interdependent living in a family. My job was to raise an adult.

Second, *parents and other trusted adults must communicate with young people that the adult world is a promised land.*

We must listen closely to how we describe our day to day experiences and must practice including descriptions of the joyous grace that comes from allowing your life to be focused on more than the self, on the care of a family, the rhythms of an office, the freedoms that adult choices offer us. We have an obligation to reveal the richness of our adult lives to our teenagers. I am not suggesting that we pour out our hearts, or break down all the boundaries. Goodness knows teens will tire of that quickly. I am suggesting that the more we can model and reveal the benefits of adult life and incrementally allow our young people to anticipate and then participate in those benefits, the more willing they will be to welcome adulthood, rather than resist it.

Finally, *parents must insist on finding their young people, and precisely in the moments when they are, as Jesus was in the story, experiencing their first taste of true identity and destiny, responsibility and accountability.*

I have watched all three of my children move from childhood to adulthood and still, despite all my deliberate involvement in and shaping of their lives as adolescents, part of what happened to them remains shrouded and unknowable. What I can say for certain is that I did my best to be present for the moments that mattered. There were so many opportunities to see the young adult emerge from the child. I know that I was not, nor could I have been, present for all of these moments, but I also know that in determining that I had a central role to play in reminding my children of their fundamental worth, of the call of God on their lives, of the mystery and miracle of love, I helped them become who they are. By listening to their stories, attending performances, aiding in study, sharing their disappointments, celebrating their accomplishments, I participated in the very transition that Will said would be gross when he saw it on slides in a darkened room but also found to be holy as he lived it in faith.

The Bible speaks of time in units: three hours, three days, seven days, forty days, and forty years. It is not important that I understand the time Jesus was lost to mean three sunrise-to-sunset days, but rather that I see it to mean that it was just as long as it took to find him, to recognize him in the Temple. When I reflect on the notion that Jesus was lost to his parents for three days, I am struck by the fact that in the midst of my children's adolescence, it really did feel like forty years, and now that they are grown and on their way, it seems like only a few days. All three of my children have become young adults, and in truth, I have no idea how long it took but I know we passed through the necessary time together.

chapter five

The Search for Intimacy

Shouldn't I have this,
shouldn't I have this,
shouldn't I have all of this and
passionate kisses from you?

Lucinda Williams

THERE ARE SOME THINGS that young people just don't want to talk about with their parents and are reluctant to talk about with their friends. Intimacy—both physical and emotional—is high on the list. But without conversation, and careful consideration, intimacy is left to experimentation, a fumbling trial and error period with potential life threatening, and certainly life altering consequences.

The gospel writers offer very little on the subject of teen sex. In fact, the whole Bible is relatively silent on the matter, except for the Song of Songs, a love poem that hints at full knowledge as the first step to true and enduring intimacy. I would like it if the gospel included just one story about a seventeen-year-old who wants to have sex with his girlfriend. I would like it if the story included a call to responsibility and a miraculous intervention by Jesus. Jesus could intervene by removing all desire for sex outside of marriage, talking about the way prayer can sublimate inappropriate desire, and making the guy promise with a level of seriousness requisite for a peace treaty that he will not have sex outside of marriage. But the gospels don't include that story, and when I step back from my desire for it, and imagine the consequences if one were included in the gospels, I become grateful that no such story exists. It would be an enormous distraction from the real questions at hand.

Parents often ask, "How can I keep my child from having sex? Should I tell them to just say no?" "How can I know if my child is having sex? Should I ask?" In small discussion groups that I have led over the years, parents have wondered aloud if their daughters were lesbians, if sex outside marriage is really a sin, or just unwise? They have worried that you might go to hell if you're a homosexual, and they have expressed deep concern about communicable diseases. I heard one honest parent say that she doesn't really mind that her only child is gay, but she knows that she will never have any grandchildren and has no way to tell him how sad that makes her. Another admitted that she had sex before marriage, and she's not sure it was a bad thing. I have listened to conservative voices explain the current mind of the church, and I have heard fundamentalists explain the significance of the wedding feast at Cana and the turning of water into wine. I have listened to young people explain why they decided to make a promise to themselves, or their friends, or the church, or God to never have sex outside the bonds of marriage. When I've asked young people and adults to define the terms: "sex" and "intercourse," they have generally squirmed a bit and defined it by talking, however crudely or reluctantly, about vaginal penetration by a penis.

Adults will generally concede that they ought to include oral and anal sex in their definitions, and when pressed, most will agree that even without any specific body part, it is possible for any two people to have an interaction which must ultimately be defined as sex. But very few have discussed this with their teens. I have listened to young people explain to me that oral sex doesn't really count as intercourse, and anal sex is an option for straight kids. Whenever I ask why kids would want to have oral or anal sex, particularly as a first sexual experience, there are two answers that quickly emerge: you can't get pregnant, and you can stay a virgin. Something is very wrong with our definitions.

Moving from Sex and Sexuality to True Intimacy

Maybe the reason the gospel is so silent on these issues—and it really is silent on these sorts of particularities—is because we are asking the wrong questions. Talking about sex and sexuality can be a great distraction when we ought to be talking about quality of relationship and depth of intimacy, the power of passion and the role of responsibility and respect. What would happen if we, as parents and educators, decided that rather than allowing ourselves to become imbedded in our culture's current fascination with sex and sexuality, we looked to the gospel stories for examples of love, compassion, friendship, and intimacy—however deeply imbedded in the text they might be. What would happen if we began to ask ourselves, "How can I help my young person find true intimacy?"

The story of Jesus in the Temple offers just such a hint, if we can allow ourselves to see it.

I know from my experience and my conversations with young people that teenagers in America have sex for any of a number of reasons: from loneliness to boredom, from the desire to have a real adult life, to the desire to have what they want when they want it. There may be as many reasons as there are sexually active teens. I am well-informed enough to know that teens are under an enormous amount of pressure to do it and not to do it. The big IT. They know that their friends are doing IT, maybe. They know that their parents are doing IT, maybe. They know that everyone in the movies is doing IT, sort of. And they know that they are not supposed to be doing IT, much less wanting to do IT. But very few of them can articulate why.

I have always thought it interesting that the media and the experts pay so little attention to the fact that young people, once they have the capacity for the feelings, might just plain want to have sex, in much the same way that adults want to have sex. Some of what fuels teen sex is hormones; some is urging and peer pressure; some is the dangerous combination of substances and only a modicum of desire. No matter which of these answers stands as our starting point, if we are to tell the truth, at least some of what fuels our young people's desire for sex is a deeper desire for true intimacy. Without the aid of mentors and much conversation, they are left on their own to discover a path and a means to that intimacy. It is not that no one talks about sex. We live in a culture where it seems everyone talks about IT. The problem is that very few people seem willing to talk and to model, to mirror and to reflect, to listen and to tell the truth until the discussion moves from what defines sexual activity to what constitutes true intimacy.

I am increasingly convinced that the more we demystify sex, the more we treat it as though it is just another bodily function, with particular concerns and remedies attached to it—like brushing one's teeth to avoid tooth decay—the more we encourage our kids to have sex. We don't talk about the heart of the matter: to know as we are known, to love as we are loved, to care for another with the quality of care God offers to us. We are too easily distracted away from the heart of the matter by discussions of contraceptives and diseases, safe sex and unprotected sex. We are missing the point. I believe that in their young wisdom, kids know that we are missing the point, and this is the key reason why it is so difficult for them to talk to us about any of it.

It seems only right and fair at this point to say that I believe all young people should be well educated in the rigors of what everyone is calling "safe sex." But, I am not sure that I believe sex is ever safe. We predictably encounter something of the immanence of God in our sexuality and that can hardly be thought of as safe. It is a fearful thing, the Bible tells us, to fall into the hands of the living God (Hebrews 10:31). But even if safety, as I am defining it, seems improbable, I do believe that every young person has both a need and a right to know about sexually transmitted diseases, their symptoms, treatments, and long-term consequences. I think every young person needs to know where babies come from. I know for certain that it is enough to tell them the facts, the absolute, bare-bones truth. We do not need to frighten them with myths about going blind, or hair on their knuckles. It is enough to let them know what is possible, without exaggeration or omission. I believe that they should be shown how contraceptives and condoms work, and both should be readily available to them, without shame. I am speaking of the ninety-year-old pharmacist who frowns, the middle aged woman at the check out who smirks, or the teenager at the front cash register who can't seem to help herself—she just giggles every time a condom package appears on her counter. All of them should be trained in the responsibility they have. In fairness, I also think that any young person who is too embarrassed to face those kinds of responses is not ready to be sexually active. Still, we must all work together to make it easier, not harder, for kids to protect themselves from unforeseen and undesirable consequences.

The bottom line for me is this: even if you believe that sex outside marriage is a sin, it is not a sin for which even one more young person needs to die, or carry a scar from for the rest of their lives. Even if you believe homosexuality is a sin, it is not a sin that one more person needs to die for. I believe "the wages of sin is death" (Romans 6:23) but there is only one death that matters in the propitiation and forgiveness of sin—even sexual sins—and that is the death of Jesus. Blood has already been shed. We do not need to lose one more young person, one more gay man, one more child to sin. We must do everything in our power to keep everyone alive for as long as it takes to find what we all seek—to be known and still loved. And I believe we can articulate these things to our young people in precisely these terms and with this level of candor.

In my mind, the most challenging question isn't whether we should use or discuss birth control, whether gayness is a sin, or whether life begins at conception or when the fetus becomes sentient. The most challenging question isn't even how will we talk about all these things with our youth, and I do believe we should. The real question is: what are we doing to prepare our young people for the transformative power of love?

We have to reinvest all the expressions of intimacy available to us in this time and culture with an unyielding understanding of God's love for us. I believe that people of faith must set the immanent and affectionate love of God as the benchmark for all our relationships: gay, straight, married, unmarried, intimate, and casual. As we discover ways to reinvest our capacity for intimacy with the sacred nature of God's intentions, we will be on the path to healing a culture which is both obsessive and compulsive with regard to sexual intimacy. I believe that the best way to talk to teens about sexual intimacy is to remind them that there is something so incredibly holy about human intercourse, so profound and life altering, that we must honor it, truly and deeply. The more we can recognize the sacred nature of being inside someone else's body, or allowing some one else to enter into ours, the more we can find ways to articulate to young people the tremendous grace and power of that kind of exchange. The more we can remind them that sex ought to be good for everybody, safe for all, and pleasurable— the more likely they are to listen to us. This is my experience, not only with my own children, but with others as well.

Learning to Talk about the Big IT: Intimacy

In our culture, the problem lies in our lack of familiarity with discussion concerning intimacy and our lack of practice at honoring the feelings of teens and children. I dare say that most of us, myself included, were raised by well-intentioned parents and guardians. They did the very best that they could, but were never encouraged to feel much or deeply themselves and were never trained in skills which might enable them to navigate and express those feelings inside the family with candor and mercy. We were raised by parents so well versed in their own silence and so convinced of the dangers of feeling that it never occurred to them to allow us the chance to talk, laugh, giggle, cry, weep, want, and feel openly in the context of our families. Most of us, Baby Boomers and Gen-Xers alike, were raised to conform, to keep the family stable and comfortable, to comply and to fit in. We were not given the necessary tools to manage our own feelings let alone the unbridled and unmitigated feeling of our children. For any number of reasons, from the Protestant work ethic to the influence of Queen Victoria, from Dr. Spock to Dr. Laura, we live in a culture far more interested in controlling behavior than in honoring feelings. When I reflect on this, I have to admit that virtually every adult with whom I am in relationship has at some point in their adult life gone to see a therapist precisely because they could not name the feeling, could not live, manage, or make peace with their feelings as a whole.

Despite being the sons and daughters of the 1950s and '60s and even the '70s, with all the ruckus and freedom of those decades, my peers never learned how to manage their own desires, never learned how to touch and feel and honor their longing, never learned how to articulate and satisfy their desire to be known and still loved. We are after all, a generation known for having multiple partners, failed marriages, affairs, and blended families.

When was the last time that we, you and I, talked with ease about the quality of our adult intimate relationships? When was the last time we told our kids precisely and exactly why we love our partners? When was the last time we articulated the depth of our devotion to one another?

Sharing Our Delight in True Intimacy

I have a dear friend in Florida who calls about once a year around the time of her wedding anniversary. She and her partner have been married for nearly twenty years. He is a banker; she is a priest. More than once in these almost annual calls, she's said, "Well, Tom and I celebrated another anniversary. We talked it all over and decided to stay married for one more year." I have another friend, also a priest, who mentioned that he was recently invited to have dinner with a couple he married. They went out to a restaurant on the first anniversary of their marriage. After the entree arrived, the husband said, "We asked you to join us for dinner because we want to hear how you think we are doing as a couple." The wife added, "We wanted to have a conversation about it, a kind of annual checkup. Would that be alright?" Both of these stories are exceptional. We are not used to this kind of conversation, reflection, and examination in our primary relationships.

The gospels are silent on the question of teen sex but full of examples of intimacy, and particularly fine examples of how difficult and necessary that intimacy is, how it changes and expands, how it contracts and grows. The story of Jesus in the Temple at twelve is only one of many.

When Mary asks, "Didn't you know your father and I were worried about you?" Jesus answers, speaking for the very first time in Luke's gospel, "Didn't you know I had to be in my Father's house?" (Luke 2:49). The story tells us, and it comes as something of a shock if you ask me, that Mary and Joseph did not understand what he was saying to them. Certainly they are justified in not understanding one another. It must have come as a shock to Jesus as well. I suspect he may have wondered how they could have missed the inevitable call on his life, how they could have searched for him for three days. Why didn't they look in the Temple first?

As for me, I wonder the very same thing. How could Mary and Joseph have spent three whole days searching for Jesus without remembering who he was? Both of them had experienced signs, dreams, wonders, and visitations that accompanied his conception and birth. Mary's own cousin Elizabeth had announced the significance: "Blessed is the child you will bear" (Luke 1:42). Simeon and Anna announced their understanding of who Jesus was when he was presented in the Temple as an infant. What happened in the intervening years? What made Mary and Joseph forget so much. If they had remembered, wouldn't they have gone to the Temple right away, at the moment they noticed that he was missing? Instead it seems that they searched everywhere except the one place they should have known he would be. I imagine they stumbled into the Temple, filled with despair, exhausted, expecting not to find the lost Jesus, but rather to seek the prayers and guidance of the faith leaders.

Something about this touches me deeply. It seems that we are so quick to assume that our young people are forgetful, mindless, boneheads, and dopes because they aren't where we think they are supposed to be, doing what we assume they are supposed to be doing. But this story reminds me that whenever I feel that negative assessment well up inside me, I might be wise to stop for a moment and remember everything I knew about each of my children at birth. When I do take the time to pause and remember, it feels a little like trying to walk on a familiar path through a dense fog. I know that I know the way, but I cannot recognize anything. I know that there are things that I knew, once, with great certainty, and now those things are only ill defined objects hidden from view, a distant silhouette, the edge of a dark forest. It is hard to remember who they were, what I knew, what I might need to know now. If Mary and Joseph couldn't remember with all the miracles and a guiding star, if they didn't understand their son, then I must remember to have mercy on my own failure to understand my own children and on other parents' inability to reconstruct the once clear vision they held of their child's destiny.

Turning to the Heart of Our Faith

But what does any of this have to do with sex and intimacy? I want to suggest that two aspects of the story may prove helpful in deepening parental understanding with regard to the struggle of teens in this culture.

First, when Jesus gets lost, he goes to the very heart of his faith. He goes to the Temple. I am suggesting that this is both precisely what our young people are attempting to do and a model for what they must do. They must go to the heart of their faith—however lacking that may be. The problem is that for so many young people, religious practice and ritual have not been defining in childhood and are therefore not salient in adolescence. The con-comitant problem is even more vexing. Even if my young people *want* to go and sit in the sanctuary of our home parish and talk to our priest, the truth was the doors are locked. The priest is likely to be too busy to spend three unrelenting days answering questions and discussing meaning.

Consequently, our teens turn to one another as principal resources for understanding their own experience. What Jesus found in the Temple was more than a taste of his own calling and destiny. He found his first experience of intimacy: individuals who were under no familial obligation to engage him, nevertheless were willing to spend enough time (as long as it took) to begin to know him.

Second, the pathway to intimacy is hidden in this story as well. Jesus feels known not only because he may have participated in yet another round of prayers and rituals, but because he, too, was willing to spend three days (as long as it took) talking, listening, waiting, learning. I believe that because he was afforded and took the opportunity to listen and ask questions, to discuss and to disclose, the pattern for all his subsequent interactions and relationships was set. From his relationship to his mother, to his friendships with followers and interactions with his foes, this time in the Temple was pivotal because it allowed him the chance to practice who he was, to participate in his own faith, to form questions and try on answers in an arena other than his family of origin.

Mary and Joseph looked for Jesus for as long as it took to complete the necessary task of reaching the end of their rope, the end of their understanding of who their son was, and to return to the heart of their faith. They had to feel the loss of their child in order to find the new young person. The elders had to stay with Jesus for as long as it took to set aside their preconceived notions of what to expect from twelve-year-old boys and to allow themselves to feel amazed by his understanding and his answers to their questions. Even Jesus had to stay in the Temple long enough to touch the very core of who he was and who he would become: a young man who must live in his Father's house. He had to stay long enough to feel the very truth of his true self.

Telling Our Teens the Truth: Sexuality is Holy and Sacramental

Rather than allowing ourselves and our young people to become fixated on the mechanics of doing IT, or not doing IT, perhaps we might hold out a kind of intimacy which must precede sexual activity and cannot be attained by doing IT. We might remind our young people that IT should be an expression of what is already real and true between two people. In this way, sexual intimacy is both ritual and sacramental. It acknowledges the true potential of human interaction. When we do IT, something gracious and essential, mysterious and important happens. The closest we can come to defining what that gracious, essential happening might be, is to say that two people become one. Forever. Amazing.

I think we can rightfully, in full faith and good conscience, tell our young people that you do not want to be inside someone else's body or allow someone else inside your body until you are clear about who you are. In other words, don't do IT while you are lost. Do IT when you are found.

We can tell them: you do not want to have sex to get to know someone. Have lunch, and meet their parents, and see their bedroom, and know what brand of toothpaste they use. Sex is reserved for the one we already know and are known by.

You do not have to define yourself and your activities through your feelings alone. In other words, you can make a distinction between what you feel and what you do. We can tell young people that all the feelings are a gift from God (I do believe this) and that gifts from God must be used and cared for responsibly. And no gift of God ever victimized anybody. When kids say things like, "I couldn't help myself," "The feelings were so great I had to do IT," even "I couldn't stop," I think we can tell them the truth. Those are convenient lies that keep us from honoring our feelings and taking responsibility for our actions. I think we can truthfully say, "Kiddo, you are lying to yourself, to me, and to God."

I think we can tell young people that no matter how much they love someone, how close they feel, how great the desire to express that feeling through some form of sexual involvement—be it oral, anal, vaginal, or merely deep kissing—God's passionate desire for them is even greater. God is closer than any human being can ever be.

If we are going to solve the conundrum of our culture with regard to sex and sexual intimacy, we will have to spend as long as it takes to learn how to respectfully discuss and honor the gifts of our bodies, the wisdom of the community, and the sacred nature of intimacy and pleasure. The church is painfully silent on these issues, but I believe that parents, guardians, youth leaders, educators, and kids can begin to have these kinds of conversations. And I believe we must.

Of course, I have an opinion based on my life experience and my faith about all the kinds of concerns raised by parents and teens, from gayness to teen pregnancy, from abortion to anal sex. I am not a prude. But my positions on these issues are less important than the challenge to teach our young people how to navigate their own feelings and concerns. We must, while actively examining our own intimate relationships, our faith and our personal histories, begin to teach young people, by word and example, how to find the intimacy we all so desperately seek. Parents also have an obligation to allow their young people to hear from other trusted adults on the questions of intimacy. In the wake of so many abuse scandals at every strata of our society, it is hard to trust anyone, but we must. The challenge is to find trustworthy people, get into relationships with them, and model trust for our young people. We can choose to make a difference in their experiences of love, intimacy, and even their intimate relationships with God.

What Teenagers Need More Than They Need Sex

Everything in my experience of being a teenager, being the mother of teenagers, and working with other people's teens in schools and church youth groups tells me that this much is true: the story of Jesus in the Temple offers us a glimpse into the kind of intimacy young people need and want far more than they need or want sex. They need what Jesus found first—a group of faithful adults who engaged him in candid and meaningful discourse on all areas of human life. They afforded him the chance to speak, to listen, and to be known. The open discussion helped to shape his expectations with regard to all the intimate relationships he would form in his lifetime, from the disciples to Mary Magdalene and back to his mother. Our young people deserve nothing less.

This is what I want—to hear
you erupting. I want to listen to you
talking to each other and to us all;
whether you're writing an article
or a poem or a letter or teaching
a class or talking with friends or
reading a novel or making a speech
or proposing a law or giving a judgment or singing the baby to sleep
or discussing the fate of nations,
I want to hear you.

Ursula K. LeGuin

F I TELL THE TRUTH, I would like to be all things to all
people, and most especially, all things to my children.
I want to be the one they run to, turn to, trust more
than any other. I want to have the answer to every

question, the solution to every problem, the prediction of every possible outcome. I want to be the wisest, kindest, coolest, and yes, even the "hippest" person in their lives. What folly. I am not, after all, God, who is Wisdom, Kindness, Cool, and Hip. But, I might as well begin with what I want. When I recognize that this will not be possible—something I confess I continue to struggle with—then I have to consider the options. Over time, that is, over all the years I have been a parent, I have begun to understand that this desire, when balanced with reality and my own finitude, can open up the possibility of relationships with others—other members of the faith community, teachers, priests, prophets, mystics, and troublemakers. If I am lucky, my children will find the trusted elders in their lives, the ones who will offer to them what the elders offered to Jesus.

To whom might my children turn? Whom else can we trust?

Adolescents, be they twelve or nineteen, need the presence of individuals and groups who are able to engage them as they are, in the moment, without too many memories or projections into their futures. The Scriptures give us no indication that when Jesus spoke with the elders in the Temple, they knew who he was. Given the texts that both precede and follow this story, I think that had they known, the writer would have told us. I also believe that had they known that he was the Messiah, the promised One spoken of by the prophets, the whole of their discourse would have been colored and clouded by that knowledge. They would have expected more of him than they had a right to expect. They would have looked to him for all the answers, instead of engaging him in the process of learning and discovery. They might even have insisted that he stay with them, and remain in permanent relationship with the leaders of the faith community. It might even be safe to say that if they had known exactly who he was, they might have killed him right then and there in order to avoid the unwieldy consequences of a true Messiah.

One thing we can probably assume is that they did not hold Jesus to his best or worst moments in the past, nor did they overly speculate about his future. They engaged him in the present, the entirely holy and precious commodity of the now.

This is no small gift. Most of us spend far too much of our lives remembering golden or lost opportunities, anticipating some next move, or next event. We forget how powerful the present moment can be. When it comes to dealing with our young people, we are too quick to hold them to our best and our worst experiences with them. We think that we can anticipate what they will do next on the basis of what they have done in the past. We think we can control how they will behave and who they will become, by relying on our interpretations of how they have acted in the past and who they have been.

When I try to consider the best and the worst moments of my own life, I hope first, that very few people know what they are, and second, that no one holds me to them. Even in what I consider my most shining moments—when I had the most fun or achieved the greatest accomplishments—I can see that I do not want to live my whole life at that level of success. Sometimes I just want to rest, relax, and simply be without the burden of accomplishing anything. The same can be said about my worst moments. I don't want people to hold me to those either. I am not always thoughtless, insensitive, obnoxious, and wrong—but I certainly have been irresponsible, flighty, selfish, and misguided in my life. What I can say that I want from my own life and from my experience is to live all of it with as much integrity as I possibly can. Integrity means that I will look at my life with candor and mercy, willing to admit that I fail most of the time, succeed some of the time, and often don't know which is which. I consider it a mercy that only God sees the full range of our capacities and, in silence, bears the burden of knowing all that we have done and left undone.

The Blessing of Not Having to Be or Do Everything

The problem is that in my zeal to be all things to my children, I can come dangerously close to playing God. When I allow myself to believe that I can be all things to my children, I do so with the assumption, in blinding arrogance, that I can actually see the whole of their experience, can feel what they feel, know all that they know, and understand all that they need to do. It is an alarmingly complex illusion. In my mind, it is at least as dangerous as the foggy forgetfulness that Mary and Joseph experienced in their search for their son. I know a lot about Jennifer, Emily, and Will, but I do not know everything about them. I know a lot about their experiences and their lives, but I do not know everything. And I know and believe that God has called out to each of them at some point in their lives, but I suspect it was in the middle of the night while I was sound asleep, or when they were miles away from me and I was busily looking for them, having no clue where they might be found.

The other problem with trying to be all things to my children is that when I interact with them from that point of view, I am likely to find it necessary to correct them too soon. Certainly, if they were to come to me and say they wanted to tell me the whole story of their lives, I doubt they could get themselves out of diapers before I would feel the need to correct them in some minute detail. It is a very difficult problem for parents, myself included, to allow our young people to have their own stories of life, their own takes on what happened, what mattered, and what they will do with the experiences of their lives. It is hard to surrender control long enough to listen all the way through to the end. It is hard, in the mix of laundry, meals, housework, bills to pay, friendships of our own, and all the demands of work and family, to find the time to stay as long as it takes.

The Time and Attention of Trusted Elders: A Gift for Adolescents

All young people need what Jesus had in the Temple: trusted elders who were neither too busy nor in need of so much control, who were willing to take him at his word, listen closely, and respond in ways that moms and dads and guardians simply cannot. All young people deserve the time and attention of the trusted elders.

When Jesus came into the Temple, it is hard to imagine precisely what he saw, but I suspect he saw space and time, mystery and holiness, all held in one place. He saw a gathering of adults. He saw the candles and the Torah, the recorded Midrash, and the room through which he might get a glimpse of heaven. Certainly, the Temple would have been larger than his home, vaster than the cramped market lanes of Jerusalem. It was not the first time that he was in the Temple, but perhaps it was the first time that he crossed that boundary from the world of the markets and the vendors to the world of the elders all by himself. Perhaps it was the first time he had ever seen the building empty, when no ritual or celebration was taking place. Perhaps he was stunned by how dark it was inside, out of the bright light of the Jerusalem sky. Perhaps he was surprised by the silence, without the cantor and the men and the women gathered for prayers.

Finding a Safe Place with Elders

What, I believe, is most important about this time in Jesus' life, about this encounter with the elders in the Temple, is that he found a safe place. By safe, I mean strong enough to bear his questions. By safe, I mean protected enough to allow for controversy without the foundations shifting. By safe, I mean well enough informed to withstand difficulty, committed enough to bear wavering commitments, and faithful enough to embrace doubt. By safe, I mean that even when he was alone with the elders, a higher authority and the history of the faith protected them all from crossing the boundaries of appropriate relationships between young people and adult mentors.

I truly believe that most of us have rarely, if ever, experienced this kind of safety in our churches. We tend to see the church as a bastion for stories of people who lived thousands of years ago. We do not easily recognize our sanctuaries as the seat of our own stories. But, I am reminded of the great cathedrals of Europe, where, on the tops of columns and in the nooks of balustrades, sculptors were allowed and even encouraged to carve faces familiar to them, remarkably human and filled with grief and humor. My personal favorite is in the south transept of Wells Cathedral in England. If you look closely, and long enough, you can find the face of a man, clearly in pain, with his head wrapped in a bandage. The guard told me that the stories of the cathedral say that this sculptor had a toothache on the day he began to carve. He put his experience of pain right where it belonged: in the church. Each sculptor brought a particular expression of their individual story to the work at hand, and the cathedral is held together not only by the stone and the mortar, the stained glass windows and the prayers, but by the presence of these individual stories.

I have no way of knowing exactly what Jesus and the elders talked about. I cannot imagine what the first question might have been or how the conversation proceeded. Neither can I know what they ate when they decided to take a break for dinner, where Jesus slept in the long cool nights, how much silence they allowed, and how many controversies and disagreements they endured. What I can know is that at the end, at the moment that Jesus' mother and father arrive and see him seated among the elders, the elders know that Jesus will have to speak for himself. They cannot speak for him. They cannot offer explanations of his whereabouts. They can only sit and watch as the mother speaks to the son, the son speaks to his mother, and they all leave together. It is noteworthy that the elders do not speak into the relationship between Jesus and his parents. They have had their time with him, and they must let him go, rejoin his parents and return to their authority.

Elders: A Gift to Parents

I have worked with so many teens over the years of my parenting. I have taught year long confirmation classes and led weekend retreats. I have spent years working with one group, and then more years working with another. I have talked with them individually and collectively in public and private school classrooms, in sanctuaries, in retreat centers, on the roads that surround Jerusalem, and on the hills of Ireland. This much I know for certain: my job as a trusted elder is different than my role as parent.

Trusted elders have an entirely different set of concerns. The primary concern is to hold out faith, to offer to young people our own faith and to invite them to find their own. I also believe that trusted elders can teach, by example and by word, many things that parents are simply not able to teach. Because I did not give birth to or principally rear the young people in a classroom or a youth group, I am not as likely to be blinded by the fog of forgetfulness, nor as driven to be the most important person in their lives. I can see things from a different angle, not necessarily a more accurate angle, but a different perspective all together. How a young person dresses or speaks or even behaves in a youth group or a classroom is in no way a reflection on my parenting skills (or lack thereof). Because I am not their parent and have not been present for most (if any) of the significant moments of their childhoods, I am free of many of the expectations and fears with which parents struggle, and I am also able to see and speak into the moment with slightly greater ease.

Once they find us, young people will look to trusted elders for a great many things. Among them, they can expect to find in us a different view of the world than the one held by their parents. They can also expect to see other ways of being an adult in the world, and the powerful outcomes of individual freedom and choice.

In all the years of youth work, my very favorite team of elders was one comprised of three leaders—the first was a public school teacher, and a photographer, and the coolest woman I had ever met. She looked cool, sounded cool, and, in fact, was cool. She knew all about movies and music, teenage lingo and slang, drug use, sex, and teen experimentation. She is only two years younger than I am, but she had this energy of youth about her that made her a great ally. The second member of the team was seminarian, a man who was about to enter the monastery. He knew almost nothing about the teen culture, but a lot about liturgy, the prayer book, and the canons of the church. And finally, there was me, a single mother at the time, with young children still at home. I am something of a geek—if I have a cool gene at all, it is *definitely* recessive. I love to read, love to play Scrabble, and like to cook and clean—hardly a compelling combination for a youth leader. But what all three of us shared, and the reason we got along so well, was a deep love of the gospel and a true fondness for our own lives. It is not that we were ecstatically happy with every aspect of our lives—one of us was ending a long-term relationship, the other longing for the stillness of a cloister, and I was tired of being alone. Nevertheless, we brought with us to every meeting a strong commitment to our own lives and a strong sense of the importance of standing with, staying with, being with, listening to, caring for, and telling the truth to teens.

Setting Aside Our Needs to Listen to Adolescents' Needs

Sometimes I think we confuse telling the truth with telling the whole story. We think that in order to get young people to trust us we have to offer them all the sordid details of our own journey. But I don't think that spilling your guts to teens is ever a good idea. Spill them to a therapist, a priest, your best friend, or a partner. My experience tells me that telling the truth to teens means that we will stand with the fullest knowledge of our own journey to adulthood and do our best never to lie. There was so much to talk about that my own adolescent journey hardly ever came up with the young people I worked with. If it had, I would have done everything I could to refocus the conversation to the needs of the young people, rather than my own needs from what feels like a million years ago. I am not suggesting that we lie, or hide from the truth of our lives, but in my experience, conversations about what we were like as teens are a great distraction from the real lives and needs of teens today.

If, for example, I tell young people that I was the coolest kid in my high school, popular, wild, and full of fun, if I tell them that I experimented with drugs and alcohol and lived to tell about it, went to parties and came home late, then I am a walking advertisement for living on the wild side. And if I tell them I was a straight A student, a geek without a pocket protector, that I was never in any serious trouble, then I run the risk of appearing completely out of touch with the strains and temptations that they face. The truth is, I was both, in my own particular combination, and so is every young person in the room with me.

Sometimes youth leaders will tell me that young people have asked for lots of specific details about their teen years. I suspect that is because the group dynamic has already shifted from a safe place for young people to examine themselves and their own beliefs to a minefield filled with the leaders' needs and histories.

Because the story of the Lost Jesus takes place in the Temple and because the text offers only a few hints at what they might have actually talked about, it seems safe to say that the work of the elders and educators, and even parents as they engage other peoples' children, is to model faithfulness by allowing for meaningful discourse until the elders feel a sense of amazement and wonder in the face of the young people in their care. How will that happen?

I suggest that there are five things we can draw out of the story which will help to describe the leaders and the quality of their time with Jesus. It may help to define who we must be and what we must do when we are asked to stand with young people in this way.

Not One Leader, but Many

The story demonstrates that one gifted youth leader does not a successful program make. There need to be at least two and maybe more in order to show young people that difference is to be valued and honored. When there is more than one leader, and all agree to share leadership, young people learn that there is more than one way to skin a cat, and more than one way to live a life of faith. The Jewish Talmudic tradition honors multiplicity of understanding, interpretation, and experience. Our young people need to see that dialogue modeled in our churches, and since they are unlikely to attend vestry meetings where there is often disagreement and difference, they can see it in the team of youth leaders.

Locate the Work in the Temple

The whole of Jesus' conversation with the elders takes place within the Temple. While I can see the many apparent benefits of meeting in people's comfortable family rooms, there is something really important about locating the kinds of conversations young people will have with trusted adults inside the actual church building. It is a salient and powerful reminder that the church is strong enough to hold all of us, our good days and bad, our games and our prayers, our stories and our fumbling attempts to understand one another. If we look again to the stories that follow this one gospel story, we find that when Jesus does return to the synagogue later in the gospel, he clearly feels a sense of belonging and ownership. It is his place and he knows the rules, the protocol, and the rituals. Our young people need nothing less than the chance to take that same level of ownership within their own traditions.

Work in the Shadow of the Scriptures

Third, the whole discourse takes place under the shadow of the Torah. For us, the whole of our work with teens must take place under the shadow of the Gospels. We must read and recite, know the stories inside and out. Of all the advice I have ever given to youth group leaders over the years, I still maintain this is the most central: we *must* know the stories. We must know about Lazarus in the tomb and the beggar Lazarus at the gate called Beautiful. We must know about the lost coin, the lost sheep, the beatitudes, the prayers, the Transfiguration, the denial of Peter, the healing of the woman with an issue of blood. If we don't know the stories that form our Gospels, we will not be able to recognize those very same themes in our own lives. If we do not know the stories we will not be able to tell them or teach from them. The Jewish tradition of teaching is all about telling and retelling and interpreting stories. This is a worthwhile construct. When we are thinking about working with teens, I believe we owe it to them not merely to be interesting and interested adults, but to be people fully engaged by the Gospels. We do not have to know what every verse means, but we do need to know that Mary and Martha were sisters who bickered, but whose grief and faith bound them together. We need to know that a young boy handed Jesus the fishes and the loaves. We need to know that only with Jesus' help was Peter able to walk on water and forgive himself his own failings. Without these stories we will not be able to offer our young people the richness of our heritage.

Endurance Matters

We also learn that the elders in the gospel story must have been people of great endurance and therefore, so must we. I am not suggesting that we be endlessly patient and always calm. I imagine many of the conversations they had in those three days were heated and terse. But what I do know is that the elders must have had great endurance. They hung in there and were committed to staying with Jesus for as long as it took. They knew for certain that if the conversation broke down, and hearts and feelings were hurt along the way, they would still stay there, in the Temple, talking and returning to the stories to find their way back to the task at hand.

Stay in the Present

Finally, I think the elders in the Temple allowed Jesus to be exactly who he was in the moment. They did not concern themselves with his past or his future to the exclusion of the opportunity that the present offered. They did not hold him to his best or his worst moments.

It isn't easy being a trusted elder in our faith communities today. Parents are often afraid of what other adults might say to their kids. We are often afraid that somehow we will say the wrong thing and do damage. But I know that when a group of adult members of a faith community decides to open the door and allow young people in, when they promise to be present, to stay and to work it out, kids flock to churches. They don't come because we have the best spaces, or the best equipment, or because we watch the best videos, sing the best songs, or play the best games. They come for the very same reasons that Jesus came to the Temple: to find their places in the world. It is our job to show them that it is possible. Every adolescent has questions and answers which, given enough time, will astound us. Every adolescent has at least a little grace and wisdom to share with us. Are we willing to take the necessary time to see it?

In all the stories of the saints, the martyrs, and the elders, the one thing that seems to be consistent is their willingness to take time for prayer and study and time to engage the concerns of the world. When I reflect on what I want for my children, in truth, it is not so much that I want to be all things to them as that I want to make certain that they find everything they need from an elder—even if they find it in someone else. I hoped that my children would find other adults to turn to. I hoped they would be faith-filled men and women who would help them along the way. Although not always in the context of an organized youth program, my children have found that. The elders are everywhere.

I think most parents worry that their children will turn to untrustworthy individuals who lack faith and will somehow lead their children away from them and away from the faith. Though this is a legitimate concern, the best advice I can give to assure parents that this will not happen to their children has little to do with other people. It has more to do with what parents must do for themselves: love your own life; gather around yourself a circle of friends, to any one of whom you would entrust your children; learn the gospel stories, and be willing to be a presence in the lives of your sons' and daughters' friends; meet and greet those elders with whom your teens are in relationship, and pay close attention to whether the elder yields to your authority when you show up in the same way that the elders yielded their relationship with Jesus to his relationship with his mom and dad. Any youth leader or elder who won't do that much ought to be reported to the clergy in charge. And finally, this: don't let go too soon. Don't assume that just because your child is in the Temple that all is well and your work is done. Even after Mary and Joseph find Jesus, they don't just quietly acquiesce to the dynamics in the Temple. They ask questions and insist on a particular quality of answer regardless of how engaging and amazing everyone else finds their son to be.

Most of all, even though I cannot be all things to my children, especially now that they are tall and grown and living lives that would keep me awake every night if I pondered them too much, most of all I can be their mom, forever, for as long as I live. And that really is job enough. Someone else will have to be the elder, the best friend, the partner, the one who reaches out and says, "I want to hear you. Ask your questions. Tell me your truth." I cannot be that elder for them. I am too busy being their mom.

chapter seven

The Possibility of an Early Death

At no time is it more
important for families and
tribes to cling together
than when someone
in the circle dies.

Harvey Cox

SOME YEARS AGO, I was invited to speak to a group of
youth leaders in a parish about an hour away from
my home. Mid afternoon on that day, the parish
priest called to tell me that there had been a death in the
community. An eleven-year-old boy named William had
been out sledding. When he came in, he complained of a
bad headache and said he was going to go lie down. Later,
when he did not wake from the nap, his parents called the
doctor who suggested they take him to the emergency
room. When they admitted him to the hospital, it was

soon discovered that he had an inoperable brain tumor. He had fallen into a coma from which he would not recover. Within a couple of days—days which were both immeasurably long and far too short—he died.

When the priest told me all of this, I assumed that he wanted to cancel the meeting. I was wrong. The group wanted to meet anyway to brainstorm in advance of that weekend's Sunday School classes some possible answers to the questions their young people were likely to ask, and to anticipate the kinds of feelings and concerns they would have. Would I come and help facilitate that meeting?

It was a hard ride to their church. I know the way, but with every turn, every mile, all I could think about what was how little else I knew. I didn't know this boy, didn't know the community, and didn't know what I could possibly offer beyond a listening ear and a willingness to stand with them in their sorrow. In fact, that is all that I offered, but what I remember about the time together is the clarity with which this group of heartbroken parents and youth leaders arrived at a way to think about all that had happened. They shared information with one another, as well as their fears, anger, and an overarching sense of disappointment. When one offered a way to manage the sorrow, saying, "Well, it must have been the will of God," the priest was quick and gentle in suggesting that all sorts of things in this life happen outside the active will and intention of God. If not, he explained, why would we pray that God's kingdom might come on earth as it is in heaven? He talked about the process of becoming God's people and the difficulty of living in faith when our worst nightmare—the death of a child—becomes real for us. It was a warning that I took to mean, we must never allow the words of our faith to stand as a blockade against feeling the invasions of life and death.

The death of a child is our worst nightmare. Nothing about it seems fair, right, or true to the nature of God's love. When adults suffer and die, we can remind ourselves of long, well lived lives, years of memories filled with struggle and victory. We may take some comfort in the things they enjoyed, the people they loved, and the final release from suffering. But when a child dies, it is just an impossible, unbearable sorrow that we are nevertheless expected to bear. Even if we believe that the child is immediately in the presence of God and all the saints, we are jealously heartbroken because the child we loved is no longer with *us*.

Framing the Discussion: What We Know, What We Don't Know, What We Believe

Over the course of the meeting, as they spoke and listened, cried and waited for some wisdom to emerge, the group discovered that they were rolling through three distinct ways of thinking and talking about their loss, and that these three could help them to navigate the same sort of discussion with their classes on Sunday. They framed the discussion this way: What We Know, What We Don't Know, and What We Believe. By separating the questions and concerns into these three categories, they might be able to remain faithful in their conversations with the young people in their care and true to their own beliefs. The framework would also allow for the fullness of their grief. It was a stunning meeting. Rarely in my life have I felt so privileged to be a witness to the ways that individuals can support one another in times of crisis.

Finding a Way out of the Confusion and Crisis of Grief

In the years since then, I have often found myself holding on to that same three-fold cord in the midst of crisis. I asked myself "What do I know? What don't I know? And what do I believe?" while my Jennifer was in surgery. I asked myself the same three questions when Emily was in a car accident while I was in Los Angeles at a speaking engagement, and again when my mom had surgery to remove a cyst. I asked myself these questions, glued to the television, when I couldn't reach Emily for hours in Manhattan on the painfully long morning of September 11, 2001. I have asked myself these questions when other crisis moments have invaded my life. But I also ask myself these questions when I wake up in the middle of the night wondering if my children are alright. Nothing in particular needs to prompt those fears—sometimes, just the silence of the house will do it for me. The joy of loving deeply has a flip side: fear of loss and concomitant questions of faith.

The horrible truth is that for all the promises of God expressed in our Scriptures, I don't find a sure promise of physical safety, endless health, optimism, and long life. So often our lives are touched by events and circumstances that are just plain hard, unexpected, and cruel. I am not certain that anything can sufficiently prepare us for the suffering that so often comes knocking on our doors and then invades our lives. Nor do I find it particularly reassuring or realistic to say that we ought to give speedy thanks in the face of tremendous loss, even though I have known more than a few friends who were able to do exactly that when death came to their door and snatched away a child, or a parent, or a loved one. I have watched, in moments of profound loss, a grace become available to the grieving which was not available to me as a bystander.

When my stepmother died, I was able to give some kind of meager thanks. She was suffering, and as much as anyone can be ready for death, I believe she was. She died as she lived, and it was a grace to be a part of that portion of her life, but I was also devastated by the loss. What I knew, what I didn't know, and what I believe offered some comfort and a framework, however flimsy, for allowing me to endure and survive my loss.

In the months surrounding my stepmother's death, the meetings with the youth leaders, and other times in my life, it became painfully clear to me that as a culture, we don't talk enough about death. We don't discuss our beliefs about the hereafter, about heaven and hell. We don't look death in the eye. We may know what happens to the bodies of our loved ones, in the literal, physical moment, but we are unsure of what we believe about the spirit and the soul's ongoing life in Christ.

I have to admit that most of what I know about the face of death I have learned from television, from episodes of *Law and Order*, or from the movies. I sit and watch, allow myself to be moved in some fashion, and trust that the writers, producers, actors, and cameramen will structure a resolution that leaves me feeling safe and secure when the final credits roll. It may be a cathartic process, but hardly one of transformation. We watch, but we rarely discuss. This seems especially true when I consider the number of movies and TV shows and stories in which death has played a crucial role compared with the number of opportunities my own children have had to talk with anyone about death—even me. But our faith tradition does have some clear things to say to us about death. We are not left with the final credits. We are left with the community of believers, the creeds, the stories of our Scriptures and the intervention of God's Spirit. All work together to inform both the loss itself and the process of our grieving.

I cannot contemplate Mary and Joseph's search for their son without recalling the late nights I have spent wondering if my own children will find their way home alive. They must have been horrified. But what of Jesus? Did he fear death, or even acknowledge it as a child? We cannot know for certain, but I do know that teenagers tend to balance their awareness of death with an internal sense of personal immortality and invincibility. As young children, the dangers are unknown to them. As older children, the potentials of their own ability and growing autonomy are far more salient to them than any impending dangers. And as teens, the intoxication of new freedom, new ideas, and new possibilities seems to create a fearlessness that can be hard for any parent to manage. It is almost a blind spot in their vision of themselves and the world at large. Despite their sense of omnipotence, many of the young people I have loved and cared for, when given the chance to talk about danger and risk, injury and death, spoke with clarity and conviction about their profound understanding of the ever-present possibility of death. They even expressed dismay that their parents didn't trust them to know these things. If for no other reason, the fact that we talk so little about death and danger in light of what we believe as people of faith, our youth are left confusing our desires for their safety with a lack of trust. They honestly believe that the limits we place on their wandering, their experimentation and their attempts at a wider range of experience are rooted in our inappropriate under-standing of their intentions. They think we don't trust them. For parents, this is rarely the case. Ideally as we age, we carry a greater litany of losses, a deeper understanding of the sacred quality of life itself. In truth, we have been hurt more times, lost more, feared more, surrendered more, and our experience informs our concern in ways that are generally hidden from our children. They think we don't trust them when in fact, it may be life itself that we have learned not to trust.

We are living, as Jesus lived, in a time of danger, of bandits, and diseases that will snatch your life away faster than you can call upon the name of the Lord. The problem is, our young people know it too, and too rarely do we talk to one another about it. In the ten years that I was actively engaged in youth ministry at the parish level, most of the young people I worked with knew someone who had died—a relative, or a friend, a kid in their math class, a child down the street. Many knew people who had died of AIDS or who had been killed in senseless automobile accidents. Once the conversations were initiated, the honesty with which young people were willing to speak raised our discourse to something higher than platitudes and well-meaning answers. We were able to face the hardest questions of all: what do I know, what don't I know, and what do I believe? In most cases, the young people were remarkably aware of the dangers they face, and, in general, they were willing to acknowledge the complicated risks of being a teenager in the United States.

What intrigued me about the stories they told was that so many of them knew that their parents were endlessly afraid they were going to die, and in response, the young people couldn't find any way to communicate to them that they, too, were afraid of dying, and doing everything they could to stay alive. It seemed like just one more example of ways in which parents and their children lack either the practice or the vocabulary to tell one another the truth in ways that they will then be able to understand.

What do we tell our young people about death? I hold two memories of brief conversations with adults about death from my own childhood. I remember the first day in a seventh grade biology classroom as the teacher explained that death is a part of the life cycle. "Death is not the opposite of life," she said, "it is the opposite of birth." Clearly this made an impression on me, as I have remembered it all these years. It undoubtedly informs my understanding of the limits of the life cycle and the miracle of eternal life. But, I also remember my father saying to me late in my teenage years that he knew I had always been aware of death. He said that he could remember me as a little child, knowing that when the dog "went away," the dog didn't just go away, the dog *died*. Apparently, I drew some comfort from the facts.

But adults will rarely offer the facts, at least about death. We whisper that grandparents are angels now. We say that they watch over us. We remind our children that heaven is a place of comfort and consolation where no more tears are shed. In these small strategies we offer images that might console, but we do not often give time and attention to what we actually truly know and believe about death and dying. Why do we say these things? It may be nothing more than our feeble and human attempts to create concrete images that will offer comfort. It may be that at the bottom of this pile of aphorisms and images all we are left with is survival in our sorrow and the possibility that after death there is nothing. While that may be all we can muster for ourselves, I believe that most of us actually want something more for our children. But we say little, if anything; we hide our grief; and we allow our generalized silence to make the few conversations we might have all the more important.

In times of grief, the community must speak. The individual cannot be expected to hold all the truths of our faith intact. Death comes and breaks our hearts. It is the community of faith that has both the potential and the capacity to bind our hearts back together, to renew in us the joy of our salvation, and to call us back from the depths of despair into the rhythms and rituals of life. Left alone, the one who grieves may well lose their way. In community, with mindful, sensitive presence and conversation, the one who grieves is afforded a powerful invitation to deepen their faith and come back to life. This is what the promise of resurrection is all about, surely!

I believe that grieving is both necessary and holy. To try to truncate the process, or to deny it altogether is not the way of our Gospels. Think of Mary and Martha, who, despite their difference in personality, shared the common experience of grief at the death of their brother Lazarus. Think of the many who came to Jesus, asking him to raise their loved ones, to heal their sick family members, to cast demons out of their friends. Grief and sorrow invite us closer to the One in whom we place our confidence and trust. As in the Gospel stories, we can use the community of faith and invite the presence of God's Spirit to come together to inform our answers to the three big, hard questions. What do I know? What don't I know? What do I believe?

What I know about the value of life has been informed by many sources: by watching my stepmother's death and by being a mother myself. But it is more than that. When I attended university, I had the chance to study with a professor who, after his final lecture on the psychology of religion, announced that he had one more thing to talk to us about. He proceeded to talk about life, its sacred quality, and the moral imperative to stay alive. He said nothing mattered more. He stressed that life is the most precious of all gifts in all the religious traditions we had studied during the semester. He said that it was important to stay alive for as long as possible. Do not give up. Do not lose heart. Do not throw your life away. This little man, speaking from behind his lectern, held a lecture hall of 500 students captive for a full ten minutes as he articulated a series of reasons for staying alive. This was the same man who had terrified his students with his stern grading policy, his demanding reading list, and the thorough way in which he introduced everyone to Freud, Jung, James, Eliade, and Spilka. But when he began to talk about death, a profound silence fell over the room. We had discussed death in the course of our study, but he was spoke differently now, in tones better suited to a minister on a Sunday morning than a Ph.D. scholar in a lecture hall at a major state-supported university. I remember this more than any other of his lectures. Why? Because he was telling the truth to a hall full of young people.

There are no easy solutions, no simple answers. So much is hint-and-guess, hide-and-seek. But this is what I *do* know, and it offers me a place to begin to talk to my young people about death. We must begin by telling the truth.

This is what I know: *everyone* will die. Death is the opposite of birth. If you are born, you will surely die. *Everyone* passes from this life through the portal of death, even Jesus. I know that very few are prepared for death's coming; it always seems to come too soon. I know that death is both final and inevitable. I know that we must learn how to take the best care of ourselves, our spirits and our bodies. And I know that all of this is more easily said than done.

But, in any particular situation, there are particularities. While it may seem important to address the loftier aspects of what I know, in the moment of crisis it is far more helpful to get all the facts and to gather them with as much accuracy as possible. In the experience of William's death, the youth leaders agreed that it was important to tell the members of William's youth group as many of the details as they knew. The goal was to answer the question of what, exactly, happened with as much accuracy as possible. This was more easily said than done. It takes time and patience to gather this kind of information, but it is essential because it allows teenagers to understand the sequence of events, the responses to those events, and the ultimate end. Teens are intellectually capable of assembling a meaningful time line and course of events that will allow them to feel assured that as much as could be done *was* done. Or, conversely, that nothing could be done because sometimes time is the enemy and the events happen at such a rapid pace that options are limited, sometimes cruelly, inexplicably limited. As we offer these details, we help our youth learn about the kinds of responses that are possible when their lives are visited by illness, sudden death, or accidents. But, despite our willingness to share the details, we must take care to pace the disclosure. Answering a series of questions will be far more effective than a forensic lecture on what happened.

In my willingness to allow my young people to see the limits of what I know about death, I must also share what I do not know with equal honesty and particularity. "He had a congenital brain tumor." "She had cancer of the lymph nodes." "The tumor was inoperable." "The cancer had spread through her body." "The doctors tried many treatments, and all the signs we call vital stopped." "The car was going sixty miles an hour." "Death was swift." "Death was slow." "I don't know why. I wish I did." I have to make room for the opportunity to tell them what I don't know. No matter how many details and explanations I gather in my quest to know, death will always bring me to the limits of my knowledge in order that I might move from knowledge, through ignorance, to faith.

What I Don't Know

I don't know why the good and kind and young
have to die.
I don't know what happens after death.
I don't know where we go or how we get there.
I don't know how to prepare myself for death,
unless it is to learn how to live.

Actually, the list of things I don't know is endless. In
approaching the limits of my knowledge, and allowing
young people to see that approach and the fear and
trembling it causes in me, I leave room for the faith that
sustains me, and hopefully, will sustain them as well. It is
the motion that takes me from arrogance, through
resistance to obedience. Uncomfortable and awkward as
this process might be for me, it is necessary that I allow
young people to see it.

There is a great danger in preventing young people
from seeing the conflicts we face—we will be trapping
our young people into the illusion that faith offers us a
kind of rescue from suffering. It does not. Faith offers us
a framework for facing our suffering and our deepest
fears with assurance. When we give our young people
the chance to see our limits, we also give them the
chance to see the potential of our faith.

What I Believe

Jesus said "I am the resurrection and the life. He
who believes in me will live even though he dies"
(John 11:25).

When Jesus died, he conquered death in order
that all people might have eternal life.

When I die, when my children die, when
everyone I know and love is gone, their bodies and
their spirits will be resurrected into eternity where
they will enjoy the company of the Godhead and
the companionship of all the saints.

For all that I know, and all that I don't know, I believe in the resurrection of the body and the life everlasting. I believe it when I stand with the community of faith and recite the creeds. I believe even when I am filled with doubt, sorrow, and fear.

And perhaps most of all, I believe that God calls all souls, saints and sinners, to his presence in love. I am jealous for their company, but I believe that at the last day, we will all be reunited.

How can I believe any of this and know that I will die? How can we learn to live with the tension between what we know and what we believe? The truth is, belief is a decision, a determination to stand with a set of principles that speak into my experience of existential terror. I am not sure it is possible to have an intellectual understanding of what it means to live and never die, as Jesus promised. Nor do I fully understand how Jesus conquered death. But I do know that my belief in these promises when combined with my ongoing disciplines of prayer and the presence of God's people in my life inform my search for answers and my quest for a deeper faith.

There is a verse in the psalms from which I have been able to draw some comfort. The Psalmist writes: "Hear my voice, O Lord, when I complain, and save my life from fear of the enemy" (Psalm 64:1). In terms of life, death is the ultimate enemy. It is the one we personify as the grim reaper or a dark angel. We fear it will enter our rooms and find us, snatch us up and carry us away. Death is coming, at the door, ever at the gate. But the psalmist reminds me it is not death I need to worry about; it is my fear of death. If I allow it to, the fear of death will color all my experiences, change my actions, and keep me from living a life which honors the power and presence of something more than this life, this birth and death cycle, and that is the eternal and unyielding presence of God.

Helping Our Adolescents Find a Way to Face Death

It seems so important to talk about death with young people, not only to prepare them for the inevitability of it, but also to open up this framework, this tension in which believing and trust emerge as the viable solution, the easement, and the only true grace. In facing the mystery of death, the possibility of an early death, and the depths of grief, we may also face an opportunity to touch the heart of our faith and begin to look at the practices which sustain us.

For years, I have been a collector of sayings—tiny phrases and expressions that I have read, or heard in lecture halls, or sung in familiar hymns or songs on the radio. Something about the voices, the chorus of so many people over so many centuries attempting to make sense of the world through their facility for language, is a source of comfort to me.

> Live then as if you are eternal.—Plato
>
> First determine what you would be then do what you must do. —Epictetus
>
> There's a wideness in God's mercy, like the wideness of the sea. —Frederick William Faber
>
> For every human problem there is a neat, plain solution—and it is always wrong. —H.L. Menken
>
> Death is there to keep us honest, constantly reminding, we are free. —Dan Fogelberg

The sayings help me manage when my own words fail. They remind me that it is not an easy thing to come to terms, literally, with life, and even more perplexing and challenging when I try to come to terms with death. Perhaps one cannot come to terms at all. Perhaps one must come to faith.

Parenting and teaching teens must include a conversation and a conviction about death. We must talk about the very fragile nature of our finite existence if we are to touch the strength and beauty of faith's potential. I must reach the limit of what I know, touch the breadth of what I do not know, and see the shape of what I believe. If I will allow it, death will afford me this vantage more certainly than any other human experience, but not without time and not without community and not without faith.

Death: The Thief and Creator of Chaos

After the death of my stepmother, my father fell into a deep depression that lasted for many months. For weeks he paced and prayed, contemplated and, I suspect, hoped that life might breathe back into him or death might escort him away. I suspect he would have liked one or the other to come in and save the day in one swift motion. But that is not what happened. Instead, the steady, slow rhythms of the sun and the moon, the rain and the wind continued. The phone rang. The morning paper still arrived. The evening news still came at 6:00. Life may be fragile, but it is also tenacious. He finally attended to a short list of projects in the house; he fixed the windows so that every one of them would open easily. He wrote a sorrowful memoir of his journey through her death.

Two incidents allowed me to see something of my father's heart which only death could enable. The first was one evening, about six weeks after her death. He called—in itself something of a miracle as my father and I both have a strong aversion to the telephone. He sounded remarkably jubilant and upbeat. In the background I could hear the stereo, a symphony playing at full tilt. He said, "I'm back, Amanda." I asked him what he meant, and he said that he had decided to cook something extravagant. He had made an orange souffle. It had worked. It puffed up and tasted like sun-colored orange silk. I laughed with him, told him I loved him, and would see him the next day.

The next day when I came by for tea, I stood outside his front door for a moment and listened as the stereo once blasted out music. He was listening to Sondheim, to the song in which the cornerstone of the lyric says, "Somebody hold me too close and sit in my chair and make me aware of being alive." I listened through the door, and waited for the song to end, or for a pause in the music through which he might be able to hear the doorbell. I did not want to come in unannounced. When he came to the door, he was glad to see me, of course, but he was also filled with sorrow again. There is no hop, skip, and jump out of the sorrow we feel when faced with death, only a steady plodding through an unmanageable terrain of the heart.

I want my own children to know how death steals a sense of surety from you and in so doing brings you back to the quest for meaning. I want them to know how impossible it is to imagine that someone you love has gone from you to some other realm, be it heaven or hell or a deep sleep till the final day. How lonely and strange the world still seems to me on some days when I realize that I would give anything to show my stepmother one more yard of fabric, or share one more Little Debbie cookie with her, or tell her one more story of the best part of my day. Ten years later, I am still waiting for the chance to sit down beside her one more time and tell her all that I remember and all that I hope for. Death steals from us but *fear* of death will do even more damage. It will leave us paralyzed and despairing.

Welcoming Companion Grief

I want my children to know that when someone we love dies, we will grieve. If we allow grief to be our companion, complain about our loss, and rely on what we believe, we may well find ourselves digging deeper into the ground on which we stand, planting ourselves more firmly in this miracle of life. I want them to know that we have an obligation, not only to remember, but to reenact and revitalize in our own bodies the qualities we most admired in the one who has been snatched from us.

Embracing Life

I want my children to know that they must stay alive. Outlive me. Balance bravery with caution. Count the cost when they most want to be reckless. Remember who they are at every turn, not merely my children, but beloved children of a loving God. This is the responsibility of the faith community, and I want my children to have that circle of faith filled individuals who will stand with them in every aspect of their lives.

Watching for the Danger of Despair

It is not enough to face the problem of despair and fear that the loss of another can engender. Parents must also be willing to face the despair and fear that fuel so many needless deaths in our young people. We have the obligation to watch for and inform our youth of the real and significant threats to their lives. We must insist on their learning to drive cautiously, defensively, and well. We must also be aware that teenage homicide is a real and present danger. Teens who have ready access to firearms are at the greatest risk. Reasonable people may disagree in their interpretation of our constitutional right to "bear arms" but no reasonable parent should leave guns in their homes, garages, or cars where a young person can gain access to them. Even if the guns are stored under lock and key or in a combination safe, we must never underestimate our children's capacity to find the key and learn the combination.

Part of the challenge of youth is learning to manage the wide range of human emotions. Despair and anger are not as well mitigated in adolescents by the wisdom of experience as they are in the broader adult community. What may seem like a small and insignificant offense to an adult may seem worthy of murder to a teen. I believe that parents must advocate for anger management training in the complex of course options available to educators, and churches would be well advised to offer comparable classes to the faith community in Sunday morning education hours.

As parents, we should be aware of the warning signs for suicide and be versed in the strategies that professionals recommend for intervention. We must uncover what we know, what we don't know, and what we believe about suicide. According to the United States Center for Disease Control and Prevention (CDC) and the American Psychiatric Society (APS), suicide is the third leading cause of death for people between the ages of fifteen and twenty-four. Between 1980 and 1996, suicide rates increased one hundred percent in youths between the ages of ten and fourteen. During the same period, the suicide rate of black males between the ages of fifteen and nineteen more than doubled. According to one journalist, Jessica Portner, one in thirteen American students will attempt suicide during the course of their education. Sixty per cent of all teen suicides are committed with a firearm. More girls attempt suicide than boys, but more boys succeed in their first try.

The research at the CDC indicates that young people most at risk for committing suicide have some combination of the following characteristics:

- have attempted suicide in the past
- have a family history of suicide
- have a firearm in the home
- consume alcohol and/or abuse other substances
- are depressed (changes in sleeping patterns and appetite, feeling worthless)
- have experienced violence (physical, sexual, domestic, or child abuse)
- are experiencing unusual stress due to adverse life events, such as separation or divorce
- have spent time in jail or prison
- have a medical condition
- move frequently from one location to another
- experienced poor parent/child communication
- feel socially isolated[1]

Often, both parents and educators have asked me for specific suggestions for intervention, as though there were some magic combination that would make all the difference. But the suggestions for prevention are hardly magical, nor are they rocket science. They are the very kinds of things we all know we can do: listen well and often, express directly just how devastated we would be if they took their own life, be specific and frank in our conversation, acknowledge the depth and reality of the individual's feelings of hopelessness and despair, make ourselves aware of the resources available to us, keep firearms and alcohol out of harm's way, and get help from trained professionals. In other words, stay in relationship. Be the community of faith that bears one another's burdens with uncompromising commitment. When Paul tells us that as the body of Christ we should bear one another's burdens, he is speaking to the parents of teens as well as to the community of faith in general.

Knowing that one in thirteen students will attempt suicide before they graduate from high school, how can parents and members of the faith community bear to avoid talking about what we know, what we don't know, and what we believe? Every day, eighty-six people in the United States die by their own hand, and fifteen hundred try to. How can we remain silent?

Learning to Share Grief

Talk isn't the answer for everything. I know this, but words can sometimes help. Adolescents need adults to help them learn how to manage their emotional lives. We can learn how to feel what we feel by learning how to talk about it. And we can learn how to manage and effect change by learning how to be in community with one another in times of crisis. At the time, if it had been up to me, I would have canceled that meeting in the church on the day young William died. But, I would have been wrong. Gathering together to wrap words around our experience helps; sharing our lives matters;

making sense of our experience in the company of others makes a difference.

When my own children were early teens, many things conspired to make life difficult for them, and for me. The specifics are not important to this discussion. The details vary from child to child, as surely as they vary from household to household. But this I know for sure: of all the memories I hold dear to my heart, among the most dear are those of my children, coming to my bedroom door late at night, long after they were supposed to be in bed sleeping. One at a time, each came to tap on the door, come in, sit or lie down on the bed with me, and talk. Sometimes I fell asleep in the middle of their stories, and they had to nudge me to gain my attention. Sometimes I could barely follow the story and would have to ask for the Reader's Digest version, sweetened and condensed: "Get to the point, kiddo. I am falling asleep." In the darkness of my bedroom, I often learned more about their real lives, their secrets and their deepest concerns than I ever learned during the Best Part of the Day stories at the dinner table. Something about listening in silence, listening in the dark, when the radio and the television were turned off and the streetlights came on, made it possible for me to say that I knew my children in the night, even when they were distant and strange during the day.

It is to their credit that we had these exchanges; it is not a ritual I created. It was in the darkness that we talked about their grandmother's death and the other deaths that came close to us. It was in the hours that wrap around midnight, when I would have liked to be sleeping, would often have liked to cancel this impromptu meeting, that we learned how to talk about what we know, what we don't know, and what we believe.

The Comfort of Our Faith Stories

Understanding our Scriptures as a source for comfort during adolescence requires that we face what we know, what we don't know, and what we believe. The story of the Lost and Found Jesus is a story I know. I have memorized it. I have studied it. And yet, there are still so many aspects of it that I can never know. I am left to imagine and to believe.

When Mary and Joseph lost Jesus and had to search for him, I imagine that they arrived at the temple with no assurance or expectation that they would find him there. They had touched the frailty of his existence, the possibility of his untimely death. They went to the temple for the wisdom of the faith, for the company of the elders and the faith community as they entered the process of their grieving. Perhaps they planned to sit *shivah* right there in the temple, rather than at home with family and friends. We do not know. We cannot know. But in the story, I find a pattern for my own journey in grief, both as the griever and as the one who must offer something to those who mourn through the deprivation that death brings. Go back to the temple— to the place of all the highest and most elaborate rituals. Go back to the altar where I find comfort on ordinary days and seek comfort for the extraordinary. Stand and determine to seek faith and believing, even when what I want most of all is straightforward answers to my unanswerable questions. I find comfort in this story and a hint at grace. Mary and Joseph touched the futility of their own desire to protect Jesus and they turned to their tradition for answers and support. If nothing else, we might consider how we are turning to our tradition for that same wellspring of support.

As Christians, we affirm a more literal interpretation of heaven and the afterlife than Mary and Joseph probably did. The Jewish tradition at the time of Jesus would have focused more on rewards in life than those of an afterlife. Faithfulness to God offered the promised reward of a long life, lots of children, and enough prosperity to live without fear. Christians generally affirm that as we turn to Jesus for forgiveness, and are baptized into the community of faith, we are given both the forgiveness of our sins, and a whole new and eternal life. At death, we will be welcomed into paradise. Some Christians believe that this happens immediately in the moment of our death; others believe we will all rise together at the last day. No matter how we construct our beliefs about the particular timetable of eternal life, all Christians believe that life, in all its complexity and sorrow, is the reason Jesus, the little boy lost in the temple, came to us. Jesus said, "I came that they may have life, and have it to the full" (John 10:10). Jesus said, "I tell you the truth, whoever hears my word and believes him who sent me has eternal life and will not be condemned; he has crossed over from death to life" (John 5:24).

Jesus said a lifetime's worth of things about life, and these are the sayings that I want my children to know. I want them to know all that he had to say about how to live fully, justly, and generously in their relationships to God and creation. I want them to collect these sayings in their hearts and set them in their book bags and wallets and pin them on their bulletin boards. But how will they know if we don't tell them? How will all our children know these things if we do not tell them?

Living with Compassion and Obedience

In the midst of reminding our children to drive safely, stay away from guns, and pay attention to despair, we must also remind them that Jesus taught us to value our lives by living with compassion and obedience. Throughout the gospels, Jesus speaks candidly and frankly about the nature of true life and the necessity of obedience. It is unlikely that he meant the kind of obedience that a puppy has to learn when being taught to sit, heel, and lie down. It is far more reasonable to remember that the root meaning of obedience is akin to giving attention, paying heed. In being obedient to the words of Jesus, giving heed to them, we can begin to see the pattern for our own lives and a promise concerning our deaths. Jesus reminds his followers, including us, to live according to a higher principle than worrying about what we will eat and wear and when we will die. He shows us a path out of fear of the enemy and instructs us all to give, trust, serve, and sacrifice for the care of the downtrodden. And in doing so, he teaches us to love as God loves us.

In talking with teens about death, it is important to talk about this quality of life, this kind and quality of obedience. In doing so, we open up the chance to touch the heart of our faith: how we live matters. What we do with the opportunities, consequences, mysteries, and graces that request our attention and beg for our obedience is all a part of what it means to live a Christian life. When we die, we can trust in the mercy of God to redeem us. When our loved ones die, we can learn to live in the fragile space created by what we believe. In the meantime, how we live is the question we must address.

Struggling to Make Sense of Grief

In the late nights that I spent with my teens, while they sat on the foot of my bed, we talked about so many things that I have forgotten. I remember more of the tone and the color of the darkness than I do the actually words. I know that in those hours, we talked about life, and in doing so, I trust that we also talked about death. I know we talked about young William, the eleven-year-old who died for no good reason. I know they asked me about death, and in all honesty, I don't remember what I said.

How we live informs how we understand death. What we believe may help to make the unbearable, bearable. Faith is no panacea for the pain of anticipating death, nor is it a solution for the pain of loss. When Jesus faced his own crucifixion, he asked that it be taken away from him before he was able to surrender his will to the will of God. I am not sure that we can expect any better of our own faith. In our fears of death and in the struggle of grief, it will have to be enough to turn to God, as Jesus did, and pray that suffering be taken away, our children protected, our lives secure, before we attempt to offer our own lives in obedience to God's will as Jesus did. It is not enough to say, "Not my will, but yours." We have to preface that level of surrender with the depths of own frail and human longings. Obedience asks that we love as Jesus loved, live as he lived, stay in relationship as he stayed in relationship, and pay attention. When we think about the death of a teenager, or any loved one, real or imagined, perhaps true obedience means that we will literally carry what we know, what we don't know, and what we believe to God, in anger and disappointment and fear before we will ever be able to care for the living, ourselves included.

I imagine when Mary and Joseph walked home with Jesus, most of what they felt was relief. He was with them, alive, healthy, and obedient. I know that on the night that young William died, I found myself profoundly grateful that my own children were alive and healthy. But no amount of relief ever answers the problem death and suffering. Perhaps the best thing we can do for our teenagers is to allow them the chance to see us struggle with what we know, confess what we don't know, and find strength in what we believe.

---

1. Source: http://www.cdc.gov/safeusa/suicide.htm

chapter eight

The Birth of Wisdom

Salvation is an everyday
ordinary experience.

Gregory Mayers

Events happen under their own steam
as random as rain, which means that
God is present in them not as
their cause but as the one who even
in the hardest and most hair-raising
of them offers us the possibility
of that new life and healing that I
believe is what salvation is.

Frederick Buechner

WHEN JESUS LEFT THE TEMPLE with his mother and father, the story tells us that he returned to their home, was obedient to his parents, and continued to grow. Over time, the story continues, he increased in wisdom and stature, and "in favor with God and men." This is exactly what I wanted for my own children. I wanted them to come home, to be obedient, to grow into their bodies, get taller and wiser, and be liked, loved and even approved of by my friends, their friends, their teachers, our priest, and yes, even God. And for the most part, this is what happened. Getting them to come home wasn't the hard part, and obedience was at its worst tricky, a kind of tight rope exercise with tension at both ends and free fall on either side. They grew taller, and more secure in their own bodies. The clumsy awkwardness that had accompanied age twelve, all but vanished by seventeen. But the word wisdom evokes all sorts of questions and concerns. I cannot help but wonder, how does anyone become wise? And how can parents serve as midwives to the birth of wisdom?

Adolescents are Recipients of Divine Revelation

The word wisdom holds within it the concepts of hardearned knowledge and flashes of insight, reflection, and experience, demanding study and divine revelation. Young people want flashes of insight, experience, and divine revelation. We want them to value hard earned knowledge, reflection, and demanding study.

In our age of modernity, with its heavy reliance on scientific methodologies and careful observation, most of the structured learning that our children do is rooted in this model. They read, recite, memorize, and occasionally work a small experiment in which they can be expected to find a common result if they will only follow the directions. With funding to schools increasingly limited, and teachers increasingly held accountable by means of high stakes testing, there is less and less room in the schedule for the arts, music, contemplation, and discussion. For its part, the church is painfully silent on the role of inspiration in the Scriptures, particularly as it relates to teenagers. We are afraid to tell our young people that according to our sacred texts, they are among the most likely to see visions, dream dreams, be visited by angels, and hear their names called in the middle of the night. We don't want to talk about the fact that Mary was probably only a young teenager when she had to face her parents and her fiancee and announce that she was pregnant. We are reluctant to suggest that perhaps our young people ought to look and listen for inspiration "outside the box," to look and listen for the special call of God.

Though in our normal understanding, people who see visions probably need medication and people who hear voices need to see a psychiatrist, we at least ought to let our young people know that in our faith tradition there is a longstanding and well documented belief that it is possible to hear the voice of God and see angels and be changed because of it. And if you do, you won't end up in a psychiatric ward with your arms strapped down. Instead, we hold out a less mysterious way. We talk about creeds and codes of conduct, prayers and personal disciplines. We encourage the establishment of a rule of life and the rigors of personal practice. Nevertheless, the stories of the Bible suggest to us that there is more to wisdom than memorizing verses and prayers. God is on the move, and God's spirit speaks and illumines.

What would happen if we allowed ourselves to encourage these sorts of ideas with our young people? What happens when we don't?

In the mix of reasons why young people turn away from their parents and their churches, one of them is because we have not told them the whole, rich story of our faith tradition. We have been reluctant to suggest that something more than blind obedience, compliance, and reverence is called for and possible. We may have suggested that it is possible to "meet" or "encounter" or "experience" God, but as often as not, it seems we are more likely to refrain from than to engage the notion that God might actually, really and truly, be calling our young people to God's self in active and enticing ways.

Perhaps we are afraid to say God might, out of fear that God won't. We may be afraid to suggest to our young people that they will be called by God, lest our young people end up disappointed by a lack of calling, or worse, be snatched away by a call of such vehemence and potency that we will lose all contact with them. They will disappear into radicalism, fly off into the certainty of their own relationships with God, and leave us, dismiss us, and forget all the commonsense things we taught them.

What I Want for My Children: What I Want from God

My personal history undoubtedly affects the ways in which I anticipate that God will or might act in the present and the future. There is no question in my mind that the experience of being a member of the youth movement, the Jesus movement of the 1970s, had a profound effect on the ways in which I understand things of the spirit. In my own teen years, I was surrounded by young people and adults, many of whom were ensconced in the Episcopal tradition, who were vehement in their believing, dedicated in their worship, and often mistaken in their doctrines. Nevertheless, the time shaped me. I am unable to set aside the notion that each of us must be encouraged to look for and find, to the best of our ability and within the constraints of God's mercy, the pearl of great price. Although I am less convinced than I was at fifteen of any specific path to this discovery, I still believe that we must be born again, in some fashion. We must find the gate to the kingdom of heaven and knock, call out, seek, hope, and ask until we receive, until we are heard, until our hopes are realized, our questions answered, our desires known, and entrance granted.

I do not believe that attendance at church, Sunday after Sunday, good works, and a nod to the creeds are at the heart of the good news of God. The heart of the gospel is more closely expressed in radical conversion—from a life in which the self is the primary resource to a life in which the love and mercy of God have become the most important consideration and the font of blessing and purpose.

This is what I want for my own children. I want them to seek and to find Christ, in whom the fullness of the Godhead dwells. This is what I want from God. I want God to move in ways that we will be able to recognize and respond to, in ways that we can understand. I want us to know the Scriptures and the history of our faith, and I want us to acknowledge the significance of the faith community as a living expression of the mind of Christ. I also want our lives to be fundamentally transformed by the knowing and the acknowledgment. I want us to be wise.

What I want for myself and my children is summarized in a mission statement I came across: "To think with the mind of Christ, Love with the heart of Christ, Act as the Body of Christ in the world." I want that my "attitude should be the same as that of Christ Jesus" (Phil. 2:5). I want us to love deeply, honestly, and sacrificially, as Jesus loved his followers and loves us, deeply, honestly, and sacrificially. I want us to be agents for change, bringing the gospel to the world without coercion or violence, without insistence or rancor, but as Jesus brought himself to the lost and lonely, to the downtrodden, to the ones who walked with him on the road to Emmaus. I want both the miraculous intervention of God and the power of faithful relationships to inform every moment of my life.

It is not enough to suggest to our young people that faith is a matter of intellectual assent to certain principles, guidelines, and rules. If that were the model of our tradition, then there would be no miracles in the gospel, no divine interventions, no transfiguration, no resurrection, no ascension. The gospels would be doctrinal lessons and a treatise only, without tangible expression. Our tradition is one which acknowledges and reverences God's invasion into time and place on our behalf—from the story of God walking the garden with

Adam and Eve, to God calling to Samuel in the wee hours of the night, to the baptism of Jesus and the voice of God's blessing; from the miraculous change of water to wine, blind to sighted, infirm to strong; from the Transfiguration to the miracle of the Eucharist. Christianity rests its faith in a particular time in history when God changed everything by the giving of his Son. Even if we have never in our lifetimes seen a single miracle, it does not change the heart of the matter; it does not change the capacity of God to do the miraculous, time and time again. Our tradition asserts that God has and will act in human history and individual lives, inside the constrictions of time and space, because love compels God to act, to intervene, to transform, to inspire, to call each and every one of our young people by name.

But it seems that we rarely tell our young people this. Instead we remain silent, unwilling, afraid, concerned, and perhaps even ignorant of the importance of including the life altering presence of God in our stories. Sometimes, though we may believe otherwise, we allow ourselves to be trapped by what we know and what we don't know. In the process, we often forget to offer to our young people the fullness of what we believe. God will act. God will call. God will come into our lives. We can make these pronouncements on the basis of all that we know from the history of our faith: God has acted; God has called us; God has come to us in more ways and times than we can ever enumerate or memorize or learn through the rigors of a laboratory's experimental reenactment of some formula.

Encountering the Holy in the Everyday

In order to offer this to our young people, we will have to find it first for ourselves—not one time, but daily—allowing our own world view to be altered by the immanent presence of the divine in our lives. This is dangerous and holy ground. I have heard people say that in order to have this sort of encounter, we need to go to the holy places of the world, and touch the ground where the saints have walked, see the places where prayers have been spoken for generations, and then, perhaps, we might encounter the living God. I, however, believe that the most important place to search for God is in one's own experience, in the neighborhood in which you live. The Good Samaritan lives on my street, and so does the widow with only a mite to offer. In as much as I am willing to remember to suffer the little children to come to me and to offer what I have to the stranger who asks for a dollar at my door, the good news of God is made present in my neighborhood. The challenge is to remember to look, listen, act, and interpret my own experience in light of reality: God's own self moves through my day to day experience.

I believe that the ordinary is the most sacred territory in a life of faith, and as we model this belief for our young people, we offer them the chance to understand the blessings of their own day-to-day experience. As we say that this life, right here and right now, matters because it is imbued with the presence of God's love, we offer our youth the chance to see their own lives, right here, right now as equally filled with grace and mercy—even in the face of suffering, change, hardship, want, need, desire, sorrow, loneliness, and longing, all of which are hallmarks of the time of life we call adolescence.

It is not easy to be young—but if we tell the truth, it is not all that easy to be old either. It is not easy to be alive. It is just necessary. And in the same way, it is not easy to trust God fully, to offer one's life to the mystery of God, regardless of your age, your station, or your stature. Nevertheless, it is necessary that adults in a faith community hold out to young people the possibility of a life defined by insight *and* hard-earned knowledge, experience *and* reflection, hard study *and* revelation. In other words, adults must hold out to young people that we are part of a wisdom tradition, one in which God requests obedience and devotion of us, but also intervenes on our behalf of our weakness. It is both, always. God calls and we must answer. God speaks and we must listen. God moves and we must allow ourselves to be moved by God's motion.

Expressing our Faith with Adolescents

The problem is that we don't talk about our faith in this way, at least not regularly, not often, and not enough. Why? Maybe because we are not practiced in it, or maybe because we do not want to be viewed as radical, crazy, fanatical, or insistent. So how do we set about doing it? How can we begin to talk about these things with our young people in much the same way we might talk about getting groceries, paying bills, getting to work on time, and working well when we get there? By framing our common, everyday experiences in terms which invite us to remember God, to remember our experiences and our beliefs, we invite our young people to wisdom.

So begin. Maybe with prayer at meal times. Maybe when you and your daughter have had a conflict, or when you have had to ground your son for the rest of his natural life—maybe that is a time to then take her hand and close your eyes and say, "Lord in your mercy, help us to forgive" before she dashes into her bedroom to cry, before he falls into a pout, turns up the stereo, or rushes into the world of some DVD game. Maybe during the prayers of the people a father might hold the hand of his son. Maybe a mother will reach for her daughter.

I know it is a radical way to live, but what would happen if we decided that every morning when our kids were getting ready to go off to school, we kissed them on the cheek and whispered, "The peace of the Lord be with you." Chances are pretty good, they would whisper back, "And also with you," almost before they knew what came out of their mouths. What would happen if we decided that the peace of the Lord was the principal offering we were going to extend to our teens?

Maybe we could ask them in the mornings as they are sulking through the perfunctory rituals of getting ready for school, "Have any dreams last night?" And then listen. Ask again the next day and the next and the next until they finally say, "Why do you keep asking me about my dreams?" And we answer, "Because sometimes God calls people in their dreams. I just wondered if you have heard God calling you?"

Maybe we could decide that we are going to stop the fighting and bickering that seems to invade so much of what we experience with our teens and instead, the next time the bickering begins, just say, "Wait. I am going to try to really listen to what you are saying and then I am going to take two days (or two minutes, or two years) to pray about it, and I will get back to you." In doing so, we might be able to suggest to our kiddos that they are not the deciding factor in our lives—God is.

As parents become willing to experiment with new ways to express faith in their homes, as they model a relationship with God, it will make a profound difference in the lives of children.

This sort of living only makes sense to me when it is set within the context of every day normal life and the embrace of relationships. Our normal, mundane lives are important in and of themselves. In the midst of doing things with my young people, listening to their music, driving them to sporting events where I cheer like a crazy old woman, handing them the car keys, telling stupid jokes, struggling to set curfews while I watch the evening news, in the very center of living a normal life in which I worry about money and the future and health and safety, cook dinner and wash dishes, clean the bathroom and walk the dogs, swim in the morning, balance my checkbook, watch too much television, complain about a headache, go to the movies, have dinner with my friends, throw parties and stay up late, catch a cold and go to bed early to read trashy novels, buy another magazine and pay the overdue fines on my library books, somewhere in the midst of all of that, I want my children to see and hear me say, "God is real, here, in the midst of this messy life as surely as Jesus stood on the banks of the sea of Galilee." I want them to know that God is speaking all the time—I just have to pay attention or I might miss the whisper of it. This kind of balance gives birth to wisdom, and I want my children to be wise.

A Life Defined by Faith

We can extrapolate all of this out of the gospel story because when Mary and Joseph go to the city of Jerusalem they go to celebrate the feast of the Passover. They go to celebrate the time of year when they commemorate the intervention of God in human history. And it is their custom. I know that I have been a fairly good parent, with a litany of mistakes and errors longer than the Great Litany on Easter Eve. But I also know that I have tried and will continue to try to frame my experience of my own life inside that great litany, as surely as I believe that Mary and Joseph made every attempt to structure their lives according to their faith tradition. They knew that they had dreamed dreams of importance, been visited by angels, seen signs and wonders. Even when the mundane demands of life pressed them to forgetfulness, they still held within them some deep awareness of the possibility of God's intervention and it made all the difference. When all else failed for Mary and Joseph, they went to the heart of the matter—they went to their faith and its tradition. They went to the Temple, and they found their son.

If we are to hold out to young people the possibility that God is real, that God matters, that God loves and cares for them more deeply that we can ever imagine, then we will look strange and weird and even silly sometimes in the face of a culture that loves its modernity more than anything else. But we will also be fulfilling the call of Jesus to go forth into the world and make disciples of all. We will be showing our youth the power of God's presence and the insights and mysteries which that presence affords us all.

None of this will work if it is forced, or scheduled, or formulaic. There must be a genuine willingness to touch the frustrations of a normal life and let ourselves reel a little in the presence of life. I remember one time when Emily was about fourteen and I had been away speaking to some group somewhere. (I traveled a lot when they were in their early teens, perhaps too much.) I came home to find that she had disregarded the rules we had agreed on. She was gone from 7:00 in the morning until 11:30 at night and left no note. She was quick to point out that she didn't do anything wrong except fail to call home. She wanted me to make less of that, not more. She didn't break the curfew. She wasn't doing anything bad—in fact, she was at the library for the whole day, and then at a friends' house for dinner, went to a movie with that family, and came home. But, she didn't call. For the longest time, I couldn't get her to understand why this mattered to me. At that point I was no longer alone and single in the world, but my partner was new to the struggles of teenagers and felt truly hurt and betrayed by the lack of consideration Emily had shown. Emily wasn't getting it. Emily was sitting at the kitchen table, my partner was seated next to her, Will was in the family room watching television, and I was perched on the kitchen counter. The more we talked, the more Emily resisted. The more I spoke, the more it was clear to me she wasn't listening. Finally, I blurted out in real frustration and anger, "The thing is Emily, it is a sin to leave people you care about wondering where you are. It's a sin because it damages our real relationships. It's a sin and you need to ask for forgiveness, not just from us, but from God." I will never forget the look on Emily's face. I was calling her a sinner and I meant it. She was truly stunned. Tears welled up in her eyes and she said, "Fine. Let me think about it and let me get back to you."

I said okay and hopped down from the counter and started making dinner. The next morning we went to church and as grace would have it, the sermon was all about sin and how even the smallest sins damage our relationships. It was a miracle. At lunch that day, around the same kitchen table, Emily said, "Mom, I really think God is on your side." I asked her what she meant and she said, "That sermon…about sin." I hadn't paid very close attention to the sermon. Emily went on to say that when your mom decides to call you a sinner and then the next morning the whole sermon is about sin and forgiveness, you had better pay attention. She truly apologized and asked for forgiveness. It was a remarkable and weird lunch.

We are not a family given to this kind of interaction any more than most families are. We are just doing the best we can. Having been given a set of circumstances that are ever changing and always moving, we must leave room for God to act.

I believe that when we do the best we can and leave room for the truth to move, for God to act, that is how wisdom is born in us. It is both a gift of the Holy Spirit and a fruit. It comes in flashes of insight, dreams, and visions, and it comes over the long growing season. I want my children to be wise and I want to be a midwife to that wisdom. I can't do all the work for them, but I can try to be a good coach.

If I won't allow for the possibility of this holy intervention, if I do not suggest to my children that miracles happen and insights can be had, then I come dangerously close to saying that there is nothing more to this life than the mundane, day to day, tangible experience. If I do that, if I disallow divine participation, my kiddos will prove me wrong. And if I don't encourage them to see visions, dream dreams, and listen for the voice of God, they may well turn to others to show them alternative ways to encounter the numinous.

The Desire for the Numinous

Young people have an innate desire for the numinous, the ineffable, and the mysterious to touch and invade their lives. It is one reason that young people are seduced into using substances for altering their perceptions and experiences. Drugs (both legal and illegal) and alcohol are readily available to all teens in America, at every level of society. Indeed, according to the National Institute on Drug Abuse and the National Institute of Health[1], in 2001, more than fifty per cent of high school seniors admitted to having used some illicit drug in their lifetime and twenty-five per cent said they had used some drug within the last thirty days, be that substance alcohol, marijuana, cocaine, hallucinogens, or tranquilizers—the list of options is almost endless. Even when cigarettes (an illicit drug for teens) are not included in the statistics, the numbers reveal a youth culture which relies far too heavily on substances in order to make sense of the world.

It would be folly to suggest that any one strategy for reducing drug and alcohol use will solve the problem. But what might happen if faith-filled adults countered the usual litany of reasons to turn to drugs—availability, peer pressure, example, and untreated pain and depression—with the recognition that living in a fully de-sacralized, demystified, and unsanctified world is simply unbearable and unacceptable to our youth? What if we were to consider that at least one of the reasons our young people turn to substances in order to alter their awareness is simply because no one has ever introduced the notion that the living presence and spirit of God might also seek to alter their awareness and perceptions? "I once was lost, but now am found, was blind, but now I see"—that is the power of God's ability to change the way we understand our lives. From black and white to full color. From meaningless struggle to meaningful pursuit. What would happen if faithful adults in this crazy time in history were to say to teenagers: "If you want altered consciousness, look to the spirit. If you want to see things the way they really are, look to the heart. If you want to expand your consciousness, listen to the holy. If you want to touch the ineffable, pray. If you want to see the mysterious, dream. If you want to understand, study. If you want to find the meaning, stay alive long enough for meaning to greet you."

Again, it would be folly to suggest that this is the only strategy, but what we currently offer young people in drug and alcohol awareness programs doesn't seem to be working all that well. We are not seeing a decline in the use of drugs and alcohol. Teenagers are out there drinking and smoking pot, rolling joints, and filling the bowls of a bong, popping little pills called Ecstasy, and snorting lines of cocaine. More than half of our young people have tried some drug at least once in their high school careers. Even if I try to convince myself that my children are not in these statistics, I cannot deny that their best friends are. Ten per cent have tried LSD. Eight per cent have tried cocaine. Seventy-nine per cent have experimented with alcohol, and forty-nine per cent of high school seniors say they had consumed some alcohol within the last month. Almost four kids out of every hundred drink every single day.

In my experience, these numbers seem right on the money. In a youth group of twenty or so kids, five will admit to smoking pot and cigarettes once in a while, more than half will admit to drinking alcohol at the last party they went to, and at least one will say they know someone ("I have a friend") who smokes pot or drinks all the time, who regularly comes to school high or drunk, who uses mushrooms or Ecstasy. This problem is everywhere. Parents, educators, and youth leaders are foolish and irresponsible if they do not have regular conversations with the people in their care about the realities of drug and alcohol use in this country. Our teens need to know that we know.

Becoming Midwives of Wisdom and Truth

The very best thing we can offer to youth is the truth: the truth about what drugs and alcohol do to cognitive functions; the truth about what God has done and will do in the world. We do not need to make anything up. We just have to tell the truth. We do not need to frighten young people with exaggerated stories about imaginary consequences. It is enough to tell them the facts.

I am not sure that any parent can keep any young person from experimenting or from trying things that we wish they wouldn't try. I am not convinced that a life defined by an awareness of God's presence promises any particular safety for our kids. But, when I watch Will get into his car and head back to college, knowing full well that the smell of marijuana is not uncommon on his dorm floor, knowing that he wants to make a difference in the world, knowing that he wants his life to be fascinating, spectacular, amazing, and full of adventure, I cannot help but wonder, every single time, if I have sufficiently commended to him the peace and power of the Lord and told him adequately the truth about drugs and alcohol. Every time I watch him drive away, I wonder if it has been enough. I wonder the same things about my girls, and the kids I have worked with, the teens in the mall, the groups of kids who hang out by the corner store, and the students in the local high school. Who is telling them every single day that life is worth living? Who reminds them that mystery is a grace? Who assures them that God is calling? Who teaches them the facts and just the facts of what drugs and alcohol can do to your brain, to your body, to your life?

Who is whispering the peace of the Lord in their ears? What more can we do to be the midwives of wisdom?

---

1. http://www.nida.nih.gov/Infofax/HSYouthtrends.html
The information here was gleaned from the studies conducted by the University of Michigan Institute for Social Research. "The survey has tracked 12th graders' illicit drug use and related attitudes since 1975. For the 2001 study, 44,346 students were surveyed from a representative sample of 424 public and private schools nationwide."

chapter nine

Finding the Lost and Found

I wanted to incorporate
everything, understand
everything because time
is cruel and nothing
stays the same.

Norman Rush

I MISS MY CHILDREN. That's the truth. Not long ago, quite to my surprise, I had a dream in which all three of my children were exactly two and a half years old and we were playing, all of us, on a grassy field. In the dream, I knew that I was being given the most amazing gift as we giggled and laughed and rolled down a slight hill like cucumbers dropping from the vine. We were ridiculously happy, playful, and fully engaged with one another. There were no distractions, no demands. We were just together, one more time. When I woke up, I realized how deeply I want one more afternoon with each of my children, with all of them, all together, little and so fully mine.

We stay in contact as best we can given schedules and distances. I am always touched when I go into my eldest daughter's house and see the life we have shared reflected in photos on the walls, the kind of tea she drinks, and how she cares for her home. I feel something similar when I am in Emily's Brooklyn apartment cooking dinner beside her in the tiny vestibule she calls her kitchen. She has watched me cook on a thousand nights, and it shows in the way she slices onions and potatoes, pours herself a glass of Coca-Cola while she cooks, and manages the task at hand while listening to me talk about my day. I feel the same sort of tenderness when Will sends home an email asking if I think that a particular diamond necklace from the jewelry store would be the perfect gift for his girlfriend. We have been talking about the "perfect gift" since he was a toddler.

Even though I know that my children are truly found, there is a part of me that knows that they are forever lost to me as well. We shared our lives, day in and day out, that time of unique luxury and strain. All of that is over. Now, we choose it in a different way. We select times to call and talk, visit, and head home.

Now, it seems, I show up in their lives in precisely the way that Mary seems to show up in Jesus' life now and then. She is there at a wedding, around the corner in a crowd, with him at the end. And it appears that I am left, as Mary was, to ponder all these things in my heart, praying and hoping for the best.

I am no longer the protagonist in the story but a secondary character, and that is exactly as it should be.

Here I stand, left to struggle through the reorganization of my days in order to discover where God may be found in among the few dirty dishes and a much cleaner house. The graces that I had become so accustomed to during the years of active and constant parenting are gone, and I am looking for a new grace. Now, I am a little lost and in need of being found.

Learning a New Way

Adolescence is hard on everyone because it requires change in everyone. Not only did Emily and Will and Jennifer have necessary lessons to learn, but so did I. Not only did they have "formative" tasks to complete, I did as well. Being the parent of teenagers meant that I had to rethink so much of what I presumed I already knew. It meant that I had to reconsider what makes me who I am, what really matters to me—a clean house or clean relationships or both. What do I want from this time of life? Is it more important to be right or in relationship with my young people? In the very same way that giving birth creates not only a new life, but also a new identity for the mother and father of that child, now I am looking for a new life again and a way to live into its calling. When Jennifer was born, I was no longer just Amanda, I was suddenly Jennifer's mother. I answered to Momma. Now that Will has left for college, I find I am no longer merely Momma, but a woman with half of her life ahead of her and empty bedrooms in her house. There are changes everywhere.

The constants are in the practice, and the freedom is in the doing.

I am learning to find a way to live with the tension between my desire to know and be present for every aspect of my children's lives and the reality that this is no longer possible. They move on, on their own, and so must I. To trust that even I can be lost and found again is hard. To learn to listen for a new rhythm of life is not easy. To move into this unexplored territory of my own life and watch as my daughters and son do the same thing is to allow for the motion of God, one more time, in completely new ways.

Last August, when Emily was preparing to come home from her summer in Los Angeles, she asked if I would fly to the West Coast and then drive back with her. We agreed that we would travel on Old Route 66 as much as possible and take our time. I had a speaking engagement in Michigan so we had six days to get through the hustle and bustle of L.A.; to see the Grand Canyon, Santa Fe, the Painted Desert and the Petrified Forest; to stop at the arch in St. Louis; and to make our way to Grand Rapids and then home. We drove in a 1987 Toyota Celica with no air-conditioning and a tape player more likely to eat our tapes than to play them. The car was absolutely jammed full of Emily's belongings. We had just enough room for our bodies and two enormous drinking cups that we kept constantly filled with ice and lemonade, ice and water, ice and ginger ale, whenever we could find it. In 105° degree heat, we drove through the night to get across the Mojave Desert. We talked. We stared at the landscape, slept in cheap hotel rooms, and stayed with a couple of friends along the way. But what I remember most vividly was stopping the car in the middle of the road somewhere in the vast landscape of the western states and looking around. I don't remember where we were other than somewhere on the road from somewhere to somewhere else. Miles and miles away behind us we could see lightning flashes and dark storm clouds near the horizon. Ahead of us, the mountains, far away and milky. To the right, cumulus clouds in tall stacks, to our left, cirrus clouds. Above us, only blue sky. The horizon was so far away in every direction. Everywhere, sky. Everywhere, the land that might connect us from here to anywhere if we took only one step at a time. If there hadn't been a road, how would we have known which way to go?

Seeing the Path

For all the particularities of my journey through parenting, I am not walking this landscape without a path. If nothing else, I have the model of Mary in the Gospels to remind me and to give me guidance and courage.

I was born into a typically troubled Protestant American family with little regard for Marian theology. I was born to a former beauty queen mother and a salesman father. We occasionally went to church, but it certainly never occurred to me to turn to Mary for wisdom. Not until I was well into my adult life and fully a mom did I turn to her for comfort. Now, I find that I think of her often, particularly imagining all the things she kept in her heart. I haven't decided if I think that praying the rosary is a good idea, or if she intercedes on my behalf. My experience of Mary and of faith and the stories in the Bible is much more like my experience of standing in the middle of nowhere and looking at the sky. It is so vast, and so varied depending on which direction I face. Sometimes I feel like I am just a whirling dervish wondering when it will all stop, when it will all become crystal clear.

What I can glean from my meditations on Mother Mary has more to do with living with this wonder and the seemingly vast opportunities and potential we all face than anything concretely dogmatic. Just remembering her has helped me live through this twenty-eight-year-long road trip as the caregiver, disciplinarian, visionary, and failure. I can't protect my children from their destiny any more than Mary could protect Jesus. Obedience asks of me what it asked of her: to listen closely, and to give my full attention to what I can see and hear and understand about who my children were and who they must become. But I cannot control any of it. They are out there, way out there, and their lives are all their own. We are not playing on a small grassy field as we were in my dream; we are living in the wideness of God's mercy.

I appreciate that the gospel writers include a few Mary moments in the life of Jesus. She asks for his attention now and then, but she does not take over his life. I suspect the same thing will be true for me, as my children move farther and farther away from me. I might ask for their attention now and then, and they might give it me, but if we are all obedient, I will do a lot of pondering in my heart in the coming years and they will build lives that make the good news of God a little more visible in the world.

I can't really ask for much more than that, can I?

Standing in the middle of the road in the middle of nowhere, I remembered a Celtic prayer I had read, a prayer to the Christ of the Seven Directions.

Christ before me.
Christ behind me.
Christ at my right hand.
Christ at my left hand.
Christ above me.
Christ below me.
Christ in my heart.

In that moment, I felt some comfort, even as a tremendous wave of sadness and disorientation washed over me. The sky appeared different behind me, before me, above me, beside me. The ground was vast and endless. The road was smooth, lined on either side with gravel and earth, then fields of brush and tumbleweeds rolling off into the far horizon. Yet somehow in the midst of all the expanse and of all its particularity, the unifying presence of Christ encouraged me to believe I would be able to bear the weight of all that was possible. This is what I learned from raising children: for all their uniqueness, difference, struggle, and success, it is still Christ in all and through all, holding all things together that makes it possible to continue to stand with my adult children, in the middle of nowhere, taking time to see, listen, look, and ponder.

The prayer continues:

Christ in every eye I see.
Christ in every eye that sees me.

I looked at Emily, and she looked at me. "Are you ready to go, Mom?" I stood there for a minute, looked around one more time. "We can stay here as long as you want to," she said. I looked at my twenty-year-old daughter and thought she was the most beautiful woman in the world. "No, sweetie," I answered, "It's time to go. We can't stay here forever."

We got into the car and headed north and east on Old Route 66. The railroad tracks were off in the distance and the phone lines stretched from pole to pole as far as the eye could see. We made our way to Michigan, to my speaking engagement, and then home again, down through the farm lands of Ohio and into the hills of Virginia and West Virginia, home to North Carolina.

Emily and I haven't really talked about that trip. Nor have any of us talked that much about the journey we made from childhood through adolescence to adulthood. There isn't much need to talk about it. We lived it. We survived it. And we know it. Like Mary, we ponder more than we discuss.

I miss my children a great deal. I trust that they are standing tall, right in the middle of their lives, looking all around and seeing Christ before them, behind them, at their right hand, at their left, above, below, in the eye of every stranger, of every friend, and of every foe. And most of all I hope that they are finding Christ in their own hearts.

When I think of Mary, standing at the edge of the Temple, watching as Jesus spoke to the elders, or calling to him across the wedding feast, or watching him preach to a crowd of eager followers, when I think of her at the end of his life, holding him as he lay in her arms, dead and gone, I think I have an ally in her, a true friend who understands how hard it is to be the parent of the Lost and the Found. I draw some comfort from her silence as I fall into my own.

Do I sound a little lost? Finding the lost and found is the hallmark of being alive. We move from certainty to uncertainty, from the familiar to the unfamiliar as we move through the stages of life and death and resurrection. The principles are the same in each stage: pay attention; pray without ceasing; in everything give thanks, for this is the will of God in Christ Jesus concerning you. Love without expectation of return.

Listen for the whispers of God. Look and keep on looking until you can see Christ before you, Christ behind you, Christ above you, Christ below you, Christ at your right hand, Christ at your left hand and Christ in your heart. In finding Christ, we are truly finding the Lost and Found, the one who remains present through it all, knows our joys and our sorrows, and asks us only for love in return.

chapter ten

Toward a Theology of Parenting and Adolescence

I n Matthew 20 there is a short and troubling story
which hints at how difficult it is to know how to be
faithful parents. In my copy of the New International Version, the text has a subheading that reads:
A Mother's Request.

The story begins innocently enough, but quickly turns
me toward the painful realities of raising young people
who will follow Christ.

> Then the mother of Zebedee's sons came to Jesus
> with her sons and, kneeling down, asked a favor of
> him. "What is it you want?" he asked. She said,
> "Grant that one of these two sons of mine may sit
> at your right and the other at your left in your
> kingdom." "You don't know what you are asking,"
> Jesus said to them. "Can you drink the cup I am
> going to drink?" "We can," they answered. Jesus
> said to them, "You will indeed drink from
> my cup, but to sit at my right or left is not for me
> to grant. These places belong to those for whom
> they have been prepared by my Father."
> (Matthew 20: 20–23)

I am interested in this story and the verses that follow it. I know that I have knelt down before Jesus and asked for favors more times than I care to count. I have asked Jesus to give me what I want for my children so many times, and so many times I have come away from that prayer time quite certain that I had no idea what I was really asking for. Sometimes I want the favor of safety, sometimes honor, but rarely have I been keen to the deeper truth of God's calling on my children's lives in those moments of asking.

What I like about the story is that it indicates the complexity of a mother's longing for her children, Jesus' compassion in his dealings with her, and the undeniable call of the gospel to sacrifice and service that Jesus offers, not to the mother, but to his disciples in the verses that follow her request. He does not give the mother what she wants, but rather, gives the sons what they need.

In the next few verses, the story takes a decided turn from what began as a mother's heartfelt request for Jesus' affection and regard, to the darker truth of true Christian leadership, reward, and ransom. The mother asks for a favor, but Jesus responds by challenging not only her expectations, but the disciples' as well, and reframes all of their concerns into the bigger picture of God's intention.

A New Answer to Our Requests

We all want assurances that the Gospels cannot give. We want, at least once in a while, just a little favor from God. Before asking for it, we assume the appropriate posture of devotion, and then ask, unprepared for the range of possible answers. When we find the answer to be different than what we anticipated, as often as not, we ourselves, or those closest to us, end up bickering over dogma and desire. Into this bickering, our bickering, Jesus spoke with a new and different word. Unexpected, unanticipated, Jesus offers a new framework for understanding the deepest values of regard and reward. In a sense, he takes the simplicity of a mother's request and uses it as a way to explore fundamental truths that form the strong scaffolding of the kingdom of God.

> When the ten heard about this, they were indignant with the two brothers. Jesus called them together and said, "You know that the rulers of the Gentiles lord it over them, and their high officials exercise authority over them. Not so with you. Instead, whoever wants to become great among you must be your servant, and whoever wants to be first must be your slave—just as the Son of Man did not come to be served, but to serve, and to give his life as a ransom for many."
> (Matthew 20: 25–28)

It is noteworthy that the sons of Zebedee are James and John, the fishermen that Jesus calls to follow him in Matthew 4. They are the second pair of brothers, after Peter and Andrew, who leave their nets, their boats, and their occupations to follow Jesus. In the case of John and James, not only does the Scripture say that they left their nets and boats, but their father as well. Whenever I read that story, I hold an image in my mind's eye of Zebedee, standing in his boat, watching his two sons, the young men he relied upon to maintain his work and support his business, walking away behind the master. What did poor Zebedee say to his wife that night, when the table was set for four, and only two sat down for supper together? What did this father and mother say to each other in an effort to survive the loss of their sons and sustain their faith?

Perhaps dinner began in silence. When their mother asked where the sons were, Zebedee answered with only, "Gone." Then later, Zebedee told the story. Tears welled up in the eyes of the mother of his children. Perhaps they tried to change the subject, until finally, Zebedee and his wife were left to listen to one another mumble and worry aloud. Perhaps they even asked themselves,

"What have they done? How could they do this to us? Where did we fail them? What are they looking for? What were they thinking?" And even more clearly, I can see their mother, with tears and a trembling in her hands, as she asks Zebedee to tell her the story again, "Who was he, this Jesus? Why did he want our sons? Tell me what this Jesus looks like. Does he look like a kind man?" And Zebedee, in the silent light of an oil lamp, looking down to his bowl of food, shaking his head, hiding his own disappointment and tears, saying to his wife, "I do not know."

This is the pivotal moment in both my imagined story of the mother and father in the gospel, coming to terms with the departure of their sons, and the pivotal moment in my journey with my own children as they move away to adult faith, adult service, and the wider world of God's call to them. I am left saying, "I do not know." But I find some comfort in the story of a mother's request as well.

Even though James and John leave their father and mother to follow Jesus, they must also have returned to describe the mercy and wisdom of their Master. Without that return and the subsequent stories they would tell about his compassion, his miracles, his teachings, I do not believe that their mother would have come to Jesus later in the gospels to ask a favor. She came to him because she knew who he was. She bowed down before him because she recognized his importance, if only in the lives of her sons. She asked because it was safe enough to ask, and little can thwart the loving desire of a mother for her children. Even Jesus himself uses the image of mothering as a descriptor of his desire for his people, when looking out over the city of Jerusalem and recounting to his disciples and the crowds the many egregious errors of the leaders of his day and the days to come. He concludes by saying he would have been a mother to them, "O Jerusalem, Jerusalem, you who kill the prophets and stone those sent to you, how often I have longed to gather your children together, as a hen gathers her chicks under her wings, but you were not willing" (Matthew 23:37).

Searching for a Theology of Adolescence and Parenting

What can we learn from these stories? I want to suggest two key points and expand on them in ways that might allow us to move toward a theology of adolescence and parenting.

First, it is always safe for us to come to Jesus and ask for what we want, even when we do not know the full implications of what we are asking. The loveliest piece of the story for me, as a mother, lies in Jesus' willingness to listen to her request. He offers a stern answer, and hardly the answer she expected, but he does not rebuke her or rebuff her devotion. Second, the kingdom of God is a strange place, counter to all that we might expect. The greatest are the servants of all. The masters are the slaves. No parent I have ever known dreams of the day when their child embraces the life of a lowly servant. We may learn to live with it, but it is not what we want for our children. No mother wants her sons and daughters to be slaves, even in the kingdom of God. The concept is so foreign to us.

Most of us raise our teenagers under the half-remembered guidance of only a few Scriptures. We try to recite the verse in the book of Proverbs that reminds us, "He who spares the rod, hates his son, but he who loves him is careful to discipline him" (Proverbs 13:24), but end up with a bumper sticker phrase, "Spare the rod, spoil the child." We might recall another verse in the same book which encourages us to train our children when they are small so that they will know what to do when they are old. "Train a child in the way he should go and when his is old he will not turn from it" (Proverbs 22:6). These two verses, which encourage structure and discipline, comprise the back bone of much of the Old Testament teaching on parenting. There is a consistent theme of teaching, training, and discipline.

Nathan hears God use the image in his prophetic words to David in 2 Samuel 7.14, "I will be his father, and he will be my son. When he does wrong I will punish him." The Psalms are filled with words of discipline: "Blessed is the man you discipline, O LORD, the man you teach from your law" (Psalm 94:12). "In faithfulness you have afflicted me" (Psalm 119:75). And similar words trickle through the New Testament. "Those whom I love I rebuke and discipline. So be earnest and repent" (Revelation 3:19). "Because the Lord disciplines those he loves, and he punishes everyone he accepts as a son" (Hebrews 12:6). Many Christian families are left believing that this model of harsh discipline is the keystone to raising upstanding and right-minded youth.

Conversely, liberal parents may draw their parenting style from the story of Jesus and the little children. When the disciples saw that mothers had brought their infants and small children to Jesus for a blessing, the disciples rebuked them, as though the Christ would have neither the time nor the inclination to hold and love the smallest ones, the ones with runny noses and sticky fingers.

Finding a Better Way: Faith and Obedience

But I want to suggest that discipline stands on one end of the spectrum of what is required to parent young people and holding them in unconditional love and affection rests at the other end. In the middle somewhere is the heart of the matter. In the middle, adolescents, caught between the world of childhood and the world of adulthood, stand in need of more than discipline and more than unbridled affection. They need the wild imaginative faith and obedience of their parents.

The transition from childhood to adulthood is disproportionately long in America today. We allow it to extend from as early as eleven to as late as twenty-six, when our brilliant child earns a doctoral degree and we finally stop footing the bill. We have left the passage undefined for the most part; it is a danger-filled labyrinth of desire and longing without the presence of Ariadne's thread to allow for exit.

We are unclear about our task in it. Do we stand on the edge of the labyrinth and holler advice? Do we turn away and trust that our young people will move through the twists and turns until they eventually find the exit? Do we pray for a favor? Ask for their release? As often as not, we curse the labyrinth itself, lie to our children about its benefits. We say, "Everyone goes through this, sweetie. You'll be better for it in the long run." Might we find guidance that insists on a better way, a way more in keeping with the whole of our Scriptures and our faith tradition?

I want to insist on this better way. Parenting through the teen years requires that we stand in the middle with them, in the center of discipline on the one hand, and unbridled affection on the other, and share in the experience of being lost and found.

Another Lost and Found Child of God

The story in our Scriptures that informs this belief in the importance of the middle ground comes from the life of young Samuel (1 Samuel 3:1–10).

> The boy Samuel ministered before the Lord under Eli. In those days the word of the Lord was rare; there were not many visions. One night Eli, whose eyes were becoming so weak that he could barely see, was lying down in the usual place. The lamp of God had not yet gone out, and Samuel was lying down in the temple of the Lord, where the ark of God was. Then the Lord called Samuel. Samuel answered, "Here I am." And he ran to Eli and said, "Here I am; you called me." But Eli said, "I did not call; go back and lie down." So he went and lay down. Again the Lord called, "Samuel!" And Samuel got up and went to Eli and said, "Here I

am; you called me." "My son," Eli said, "I did not call; go back and lie down." Now Samuel did not yet know the Lord: The word of the Lord had not yet been revealed to him. The Lord called Samuel a third time, and Samuel got up and went to Eli and said, "Here I am; you called me." Then Eli realized that the Lord was calling the boy.
So Eli told Samuel, "Go and lie down, and if he calls you, say, 'Speak, Lord, for your servant is listening.'" So Samuel went and lay down in his place. The Lord came and stood there, calling as at the other times, "Samuel! Samuel!" Then Samuel said, "Speak, for your servant is listening."

The story requires some contextual information in order for me to rely on it in the way that I do. First, Samuel's mother, Hannah, was a woman of faith and prayer. Eli was a priest in the temple. Long before Samuel was born, Eli watched as Hannah came to the temple to pray for a child. Eli was not a particularly good man, but having been born into a lineage of temple keepers, he did his job as best he could. His own children were far less admirable and would not make worthy keepers of the sacred space. Eli did his job, and tried to continue the lineage of his forefathers. One day, when Hannah was in the temple, Eli looked over and saw this woman with her eyes half closed, moving her lips, swaying a little and not speaking aloud. Eli did not understand what she was doing. He assumed she was drunk and asked her to leave. Hannah explained that she wasn't drunk, but praying from the heart, from the place all mothers know, where there are words and desires, but little sound. He rebuked her and asked her to leave. Yet Hannah was insistent, explaining that she was not drunk, only praying out of her own sorrow and anguish. In a moment of compassion, Eli offered her a blessing: that God honor her prayers and give her the desire of her heart.

Soon, Hannah' gave birth to a child, and in her gratitude, offered the child to the temple, in order that he might live there and grow up under Eli's care. She gave her small son to Eli to rear. Every year she brought young Samuel a new little robe to wear and from that distant vantage watched and prayed as her son's childhood was spent in the temple. Again, Eli blessed the faithfulness of Hannah and her husband, and Hannah gave birth to three sons and two daughters, while her first-born remained in the temple with Eli. Eli cared for Samuel as though he were his own son, while he rebuked and warned his own sons, telling them that they had left the call of God. He asked them to consider if they left their work as priests in the temple, who would intercede for them in their sin? They were supposed to come follow in his footsteps and be the new keepers of the temple. The sons would have none of it, disregarding the warnings of their father. God sent a prophet to Eli, promising that while his own sons would disappoint him and meet a dark end, there would be one who came to be a true priest in the temple.

It is into this context that the Lord calls to Samuel. And it is in this context that Eli realizes that the Lord is calling.

There is always the danger of over-interpreting stories like this one. The implications are many, and the possible interpretations abound. While we may want the story to speak to our behaviors, it is only a guideline for our character and our intentions. In this story of hope, disappointment, and faithfulness, parents and those who care for teens can see a few helpful hints on how we might address the adolescence of our own children.

First, in the midst of the life of Eli, and in his attempts to be faithful, there were great disappointments and many mistakes.

The same is true for us. I don't believe for a moment that we will get through the raising of our own children, or those in our care, without moments when we mistake prayers for drunkenness, and the voice of God for a silly dream. Even the most faithful parents are aware of the possibility that their own children will be more like Eli's disobedient sons than the child Samuel. There are so many things we cannot control. Sometimes, even the best intentions are not enough. I wish I could say that we can secure the future of all of our children, but we cannot. What we can do, is continue to practice our own rituals and our own beliefs, telling the truth to our youth in the hopes that they will be able to hear it. As a parent, I feel great sympathy for Eli. What happened in the raising of his sons that made them so arrogant and disobedient? What went wrong? The story does not tell us.

I also feel great admiration for Hannah, who took the criticism of the priest in the temple and stood her ground. She received her blessing and was given a child. My understanding is strained when she offers her child to the temple and to the care of Eli—a man known for having untrustworthy sons. It must have been an impossibly hard day for Hannah when she realized that her child had a destiny which she could either resist or facilitate. It is this moment, when her character and her faith are revealed, that calls to me. The behavior of giving her child to the temple is unthinkable; the faith and fortitude of her person are not.

This story holds many precursor images for the coming of Jesus into the world and his journey into the Temple which has guided our thoughts in this book. Samuel is described as continuing "to grow in stature and in favor with God and with men" (1 Samuel 2:26). He is lost to his mother and found in the temple. He becomes a priest and prophet in the community, but not without cost to his family. Luke undoubtedly knew this story when he wrote about the Lost and Found Jesus, and the faithfulness of Hannah and Eli informed his understanding of it.

While all the stories of the Bible have great particularity to them, our task is to learn how to be in the lives we live based on the faith and folly of the characters in these stories. They remind me that it is never too late to call upon God when it comes to the lives of our children. We must pray for them, long for them, and ultimately, whether at two or twenty, we must let them go to the Temple.

This is the middle ground, somewhere between harsh discipline and endless love. It is the moment when those two extremes fold in on themselves and create a new way of being in me. It is the way of compassion and faith. It is the moment when I determine that my child is truly God's own child. When we, as parents, receive the middle ground of compassion and obedience into our hearts, it will mold the ways in which we will interact with our young people. Neither discipline alone, nor affection, can suffice. We must be obedient.

Becoming Like Eli, Becoming Like Hannah

Both Hannah and Eli demonstrate different ways that we may be called upon to act in faith with regard to our children's lives. Hannah demonstrates the absolute surrender of a mother's concern. She offers her son, completely and absolutely to the care of the Lord. I cannot imagine any scenario in which I would be willing to literally give my child to the church. But I can extrapolate a willingness to see that all of my children belong to God far more than they will ever belong to me. Their destinies are unknown to me and to them, but my responsibility is to be like Hannah; not to be her, or to try to create a life in which her actions become my actions, but rather, a willingness to be like her—defined by prayer and standing in the middle distance as God moves through the lives of my children. It could not have been easy for her, and I am confident that her life was filled with doubt—but she did not allow that doubt to paralyze her. She chose obedience and sacrifice, and so must I.

I hold Hannah's image close to the images I have of Mary. Mary gave her son to God as well, surrendering her desire for new wine at a wedding to allow the greater loss of her son for the redemption of the world. Parenting requires a kind of imaginative willingness. We do all that we can, as Hannah did and as Mary did.

But there is more. Parents must also have the imagination of Eli. The willingness to realize in the middle of the night that God is calling. That is the primary reality that we must recognize, affirm, and even engender in the lives of our teens. No mother wants her son to be a martyr or a saint. We want them to be the parents of our grandchildren and to live safe, comfortable, and happy lives. But in every single story of a mother and child, a teacher and a student, every single one, the lesson is one of sacrifice and obedience, of faith and compassion. What I want for my children is limited by my experience of the world and the passion of my love for them. I must allow for the possibility of something greater: God's intentions and God's love. I must tell the truth and get out of its way.

That's what Eli did when he told Samuel to go back and lie down in the same place and when the Truth spoke again, answer it willingly. I would have been just as likely, without this story to guide me, to call Samuel out of his bad dream, and let him snuggle down next to me and sleep. I would have tried to secure him a place at the right hand of God.

When I reflect on the stories in our Scriptures that speak about parenting, what I realize is that mothers and fathers are in the precarious position of loving their sons and daughters with passion and also releasing their sons and daughters to a passion far greater, the passion of Jesus himself, revealed and demonstrated in the saints and the martyrs, the prophets and the disciples.

Releasing Our Children to the Call of God

The story of the mother's request is poignant precisely because her intuition was right. James and John had sacrificed a great deal in their love of the Teacher, and even more was still to come. Luke tells us in the Acts of the Apostles that James is martyred. His mother is nowhere to be seen. It is poignant because she wanted for him and his brother what we all want for our children—safety and reward for obedience. I have to believe that John and James and all the martyrs of the faith will be seated mighty close to Jesus at the last day, even if they don't get to sit at his right and left hands. In truth, I want much the same thing for my own children—that they have so powerful a connection with God in Christ Jesus that I am left having to bow before him on their behalf and ask a favor—even if I am wrong in the asking.

I have to be like Eli—willing to hear my children's questions and willing to realize when God is calling. Even in the times when I may have to admit that I have failed in some aspect of my own parenting, I must remember Eli, who was willing to listen for the call of God on the lives of another father's child. I have to be like Hannah—willing to sacrifice the beloved child in order that the whole world might be changed by the offering he brings to his adult life. I have to be like Mary—willing to love my children deeply and also willing to let them go.

It is remarkably difficult to be this kind of parent. Without assurance about their futures, we raise up our children in obedience to the call of the Gospel. It is a lie to think that the Kingdom of God guarantees that our children will come to sit at the right and left hands of Jesus. The Christian life will bring them to sacrifice, to obedience, to service, and perhaps even to suffering. It will raise them up to change the world at great expense to them, and to us. Who would want that for their kids? Hannah did. Eli did. Mary did. And in the quiet of the middle of the night, it is what many of us want. It is what I want. Even when I don't know the fullness of what I am asking for.

The Path of Joy and Compassion

There is one more thing. Following Jesus in his path of obedience, like following in the footsteps of Mary, Hannah, and Eli, is also a path of remarkable joy and meaning. The more we, as parents, lean into this way of life—that yields for questions, engages stories, listens in the middle of the night for the wisdom of our dreams, laughs at our own frailty and embraces new possibilities in the midst of our grieving—the deeper and more abundantly joyous our experience of the everyday lives we are living becomes. I know this from my experience. The way of obedience and compassion brings the Kingdom of God, which while structured in ways far removed from my understanding, is still a Kingdom of joy and delight. In this way, I hope I model the truly good news of God.

We need a working theology for raising our children from childhood to adulthood, and certainly greater minds than mine will have to address this work. But this much I know and believe: Jesus said, "I came that they may have life, and have it abundantly" (John 10:10). Isn't that want we want for our children? Abundant life? How do we get it? By living as the Lost and Found ourselves. Lost in our love for God and found in his kingdom. Lost in the quandary of being faithful parents and found in the stories of our faith. Lost in the moment, more often than not, and found in the eternal love and life of God. Even when life—and all its demands—frightens us, staggers us, leaves us asking for yet more mercy, we believe something more. Perhaps the next time I am lost in my desires for my young adult children, I will remember to ask that God grant not what I want, but what my children need. And once in a while, I trust, I pray they will need me.